THE WORD INVITES

The Word Invites

A Spiritual Theology

Aidan Nichols, OP

GRACEWING

First published in England in 2019
by
Gracewing
2 Southern Avenue
Leominster
Herefordshire HR6 0QF
United Kingdom
www.gracewing.co.uk

All rights reserved

No part of this publication may be reproduced, stored in a retrieval system, or transmitted in any form or by any means, electronic, mechanical, photocopying, recording or otherwise, without the written permission of the publisher.

© 2019, The Trustees of the English Province of the Order of Preachers

The publishers have no responsibility for the persistence or accuracy of URLs for websites referred to in this publication, and do not guarantee that any content on such websites is, or will remain, accurate or appropriate.

ISBN 978 085244 907 3

Typeset by Word and Page, Chester, UK
Cover design by Bernardita Peña Hurtado
Front cover icon: The Creation of Light
used with the kind permission of the iconographer, Michael Kapeluck

Contents

Preface	vii
1. The Word of God as Source	1
2. The Liturgy as the Context	13
3. Meditation and Contemplation	33
4. Principles of Asceticism	51
5. Asceticism: Monastic, Lay and 'Pastoral'	69
6. Purification	87
6. Illumination	105
6. Union	121
Bibliography	130

Preface

This is a study of spiritual theology, and so a reflection on the spiritual life as found in Christianity, and more specifically in the Christianity of the Great Church — the undivided Church of the Fathers of East and West. Christian spirituality embodies in personal living the biblical revelation received in the Church of the Fathers and transmitted to its successors in every age. Like everything else in Christian doctrine and practice, Christian spirituality depends on Scripture and Tradition, which are the two intrinsically inter-related ways in which that revelation is communicated over time.

There has been much discussion in the modern period, especially in the 1960s, as to whether the Roman Catholic Church should be said to have one spirituality or many. Even those who emphasize many spiritualities — as became more common in the Latin West with the revival of the religious orders in the nineteenth century — might agree that to exaggerate the difference between the various 'schools' is not a good idea.[1] In the mid-1950s the Swiss theologian

---

[1] Here historical surveys are obviously essential; see, for instance, Bernard McGinn, *The Foundations of Mysticism. Origins to the Fifth Century* (New York: Crossroad, 1991); Bernard McGinn, *The Growth of Mysticism. Gregory the Great through the Twelfth Century* (New York: Crossroad, 1994); Bernard McGinn, John Meyendorff and Jean Leclerq (eds.), *Christian Spirituality. Origins to the Twelfth Century* (London: SCM, 1989); Jill Raitt, Bernard McGinn and John Meyendorff (eds.), *Christian Spirituality. High Middle Ages and Reformation* (London: SCM, 1989); Louis Dupré and Don E. Saliers (eds.), *Christian Spirituality. Post-Reformation and Modern* (London: SCM, 1990).

Hans Urs von Balthasar noticed how 'the different theological emphases of the various religious orders are increasingly influencing each other and creating a single whole'.[2] If such mutual borrowing was (and is) possible, might there perhaps be a common basis for spiritualities—let us venture to call it the 'spirituality of the Gospel in the Church'—even if to claim there is fundamentally only one authentic spirituality could be a step too far. A step too far, since, in the words of Jean Daniélou, the Jesuit patristic scholar and theological adviser to bishops at the Second Vatican Council, spiritualities—notice the deliberately plural language—are 'inspirations aroused by the Spirit in the Church' and, as such, are 'essential expressions of her vitality'.[3] That implies there are many spiritualities, or at least quite a few.

Daniélou wrote these words in 1962 by way of criticism of a book which, though in some ways *passé*, remains an inspirational guide to spiritual theology from the great period that immediately preceded the Second Vatican Council. That book is *Introduction à la vie spirituelle* by the French Oratorian theologian and historian of spirituality Louis Bouyer, originally published in 1960 and several times reprinted as well as translated into a variety of languages.[4] Much of

---

[2] Hans Urs von Balthasar, *Prayer*. English trans. (San Francisco: Ignatius, 1986), p. 151. The German original was published in 1955.

[3] Jean Daniélou, 'À propos d'une introduction à la vie spirituelle', *Études* 94 (1962), pp. 270–4, and here at p. 272.

[4] Louis Bouyer, *Introduction à la vie spirituelle. Précis de théologie ascétique et mystique* (Paris: Desclée, 1960). The English translation appeared originally as *Introduction to Spirituality* (London: Darton, Longman and Todd, 1961). It is the original English (British) edition which will be cited here.

Bouyer's text is eminently retrievable and will be generously drawn on here.

For Daniélou, what, in *Introduction à la vie spirituelle*, Bouyer took to be the spirituality of the Church was really 'his own spirituality which he would claim to impose on the Church as a whole'.[5] This was a serious charge, robustly responded to at the time by Bouyer in the pages of the French Jesuit journal *Études* where Daniélou's criticism had appeared.[6]

Three years later, in 1965, von Balthasar, while not mentioning the spat between Bouyer and Daniélou in so many words, returned to the key disputed issue in an article in the series 'Concilium' (then still in its orthodox early phase) under the title 'The Gospel as Norm and Test of all Spirituality in the Church'.[7] As the title of that essay suggests, von Balthasar in effect supported Bouyer. There is only one Gospel, so there can only be, fundamentally, one evangelical spirituality, however many shapes it may take in different contexts. Von Balthasar speaks in this connexion of the 'christological centre' where 'all possible forms of Christian spirituality meet and so, through the medium of faith, flow into each other'.[8] Although, beginning with different holy figures in the New Testament, various saints have indeed embodied different charisms, gifts that in turn have originated 'various applications of the Christian way of life',[9] neverthe-

[5] Daniélou, 'La vie spirituelle', p. 272.
[6] Louis Bouyer and Jean Daniélou, 'Correspondance', in Daniélou, 'La vie spirituelle', pp. 411–15
[7] Hans Urs von Balthasar, 'The Gospel as Norm and Test of all Spirituality in the Church', in *Spirituality in Church and World*, ed. Christian Duquoc and Claude Geffré. Concilium 9.1 (New York: Paulist Press, 1965), pp. 5–13.
[8] *Ibid.*, p. 10.
[9] *Ibid.*, p. 12.

less, antecedent to all such diversity, there is only one fundamental Christian charism, which is, then, prior to all differentiation. Von Balthasar describes it as the charism of the Church herself, she who is the Bride of Christ, with an attitude taken from the New Eve, the Blessed Virgin Mary. Mary's response, 'Behold the handmaid of the Lord; be it done to me according to thy Word (Luke 1:38)', expresses 'the true and general attitude which underlies all individual charismata'.[10] This foundational attitude of receptivity to the Word, concludes von Balthasar, must be regarded, then, as what he terms the 'spirituality of all spiritualities'.[11] It expresses the basic orientation of mind and heart which various spiritualities can only re-express with some special emphases of their own. This echoed Bouyer not just in that it spoke of one basic spirituality but also because it thought of that spirituality in terms of response to the Word. The Dominican tradition, it may be noted in passing, is especially ready to enter into symbiosis here.[12]

In this Balthasarian perspective, then, Bouyer was justified, over against Daniélou, in seeking to uncover the basic spirituality of the entire Church—which is not

---

[10] *Ibid.* p. 11.
[11] *Ibid.* A similar 'line' (there is only one spirituality in which the spiritualities participate) was taken by the Benedictine historian of spirituality, co-author with Bouyer of *Histoire de la spiritualité chrétienne*, 3 vols. (Paris 1960–1), in the same issue of this journal: see François Vandenbroucke, 'Spirituality and Spiritualities', in *Spirituality in Church and World*, ed. Christian Duquoc and Claude Geffré. Concilium 9.1 (New York: Paulist Press, 1965), pp. 25–33.
[12] See, for instance, Guy Bedouelle, OP, *Saint Dominic. The Grace of the Word*. English trans. (San Francisco: Ignatius, 1987); Aidan Nichols, OP, 'The Spirituality of the Dominicans', in his *Scribe of the Kingdom. Essays on Theology and Culture* (London: Sheed and Ward, 1994), II, pp. 199–206.

of course to say he was successful in this endeavour in every respect. Yet by and large, Bouyer's version of this overall approach is surely on the right lines. Like von Balthasar, he puts docility to the God who speaks through his Word in first place, but he also points out further constitutive dimensions of the foundational 'spirituality of the Church'. In his footsteps, I shall be describing Christian spirituality as essentially biblical, liturgical, ascetical and mystical. More specifically, Christian spirituality is biblical in its source, it is liturgical in its context, it is ascetical in its development, and it is mystical in its outcome. 'Mystical' is a strong word, but the Dominican school does not accept the opinion that this final issue of spirituality is extra-ordinary in anything other than a statistical sense. In the words of Réginald Garrigou-Lagrange, theologically speaking it is 'eminent, but normal'.[13] These four adjectives—biblical, liturgical, ascetical and mystical—explain the structure of the present book and its contents too.

It may be noticed that, rather like the anonymous 'Monk of the Eastern Church' who produced that little classic *Orthodox Spirituality*,[14] I have attempted here a fusion of sources, Catholic and Orthodox, Latin and Byzantine.

Blackfriars, Cambridge
Easter 2019

---

[13] Réginald Garrigou-Lagrange, OP, *Les trois âges de la vie intérieure, prélude de celle du ciel*, 2 vols. (Paris: Éditions du Cerf, 1948), I, p. 15. This work has an English translation not available to me, *The Three Ages of the Interior Life: Prelude of Life Eternal*, 2 vols. (St Louis, MO: Herder, 1947–8).

[14] A Monk of the Eastern Church [Lev Gillet], *Orthodox Spirituality* (London: Fellowship of Saint Alban and Saint Sergius, 1974).

O God, I pray, let me know and love You, so that I may rejoice in You. And if I cannot in this life fully, let me advance day by day until the point of fullness comes

St Anselm, *Proslogion*, 26.

✢ 1 ✢

The Word of God as Source

IN KEEPING WITH THE CLAIMS both recorded and accepted in my Preface, I consider first the Word of God as Source.

What is the 'Word of God'?

In the reformed Roman liturgy when the Scripture is read out the reader ends by acclaiming the text as *Verbum Dei*, 'the Word of God'. The title 'the Word of God' can indeed be applied to the text of Scripture, but this is only in a derivative or secondary way. In a more original and primary sense, and thus in a more important sense, Scripture is not the Word itself so much as it is our principal witness to that Word. For 'the Word' is first and foremost God: the self-revealing God who comes out of his concealment so as to communicate with us, doing so by the gracious disclosure of his plan in history. Despite the holiness of what is called (with good reason) '*Sacred* Scripture', a holiness bound up with the gift of inspiration made to the biblical authors, Christianity is not the religion of a book. Christianity is the religion of the Word, with a capital 'W' — the religion of God himself coming forth from his hiddenness so as to communicate with us. It is because the living divine Word is the central reality of Christianity that the Scriptures which attest that Word are so crucial for us, so crucial that they can even borrow the Word's name.

I have used the phrase 'communicate with us' twice. But who might be the 'us' — the 'we' — I have in mind? In the first place, the 'we' is humanity as divinely addressed in Israel and in the new Israel that is the Church. That communication to a corporate recipient is the primary concern of fundamental and dogmatic theology. 'Fundamental' theology and 'dogmatic' theology investigate respectively the *manner* in which God communicates with Israel and the Church (that is fundamental theology) and likewise the *content* of that communication (and that is dogmatic theology). But the 'we' is also each one of us, each believer, each individual concentration, so to say, of Israel and the New Israel. And that inter-personal relation between the living Word and oneself — *my*self — is the primary concern of ascetical and mystical theology. When ascetical and mystical theology are considered not just in their development and outcome for the individual, but also — and above all — in their source and context, then we can say *the inter-personal relationship between the living Word and myself is the primary concern of Christian spirituality in its entirety*, the Christian spirituality that is biblical in its source, liturgical in its context, ascetical in its development, and mystical in its outcome.

In this definition of the primary concern of Christian spirituality, the phrase 'inter-personal relation' is clearly crucial. The Word that is Scripture, in disclosing to me the living Word of the self-revealing God, presents me not with an 'It' or even a 'Him', but with a 'Thou'. That is, it presents me with One who, while intimately present to me as my Creator, Redeemer and Consummator, also stands over against me as Another, a *Vis-à-vis*, whom I can and should address. Address is the form of speech we employ when using language *to persons in their presence*, rather than about either objects or persons in their absence. The One with whom Scripture presents me is not simply One who is present in my own depths whether by nature—as my Creator—or by grace—as my Redeemer and Consummator. God stands to my 'I' (capital 'I') as a 'Thou', a 'You'. And since in his self-revelation he shows himself to be a Trinitarian God, he is, moreover, a tri-hypostatic Thou or You, a Thou or You in three hypostases. The divine Personality is analogous to human personality, it is not identical with it. No human personality is three-in-one.

Of course in theory any religious philosophy or non-Christian religion might find some sort of 'triad' in God—this claim is sometimes made for Neo-Platonism and also for one major variety of Hinduism. But it is distinctive of Christianity, and therefore of Christian spirituality, to say that God makes himself known to me above all in an utterly unique case of 'triadicity': the Trinitarian Son, the Jesus Christ who took our humanity so as to reveal the Father by the Holy Spirit, and with that disclosure revealed likewise the essential inter-connectedness of Father, Son and Spirit, both in God and in God's outreach to ourselves.

The Son has an eternal revelatory purpose. Through Him all things were created (Colossians 1:16–17), so he was already the One in whom creation could glimpse, through the beauty spread abroad by his Spirit, the glory of the Father. In his incarnation, he became the open revelation of the Holy Trinity. Here the phrase 'the Word' gains fresh meaning. For the New Covenant, the Word of God is known to be more especially the second Trinitarian Person, eternally co-defined by his relations with the Father and the Spirit and now in time, in the mysteries of the Annunciation and the Nativity, made flesh for our sake.

This outreach of the divine Trinity in search of us through the Son is more defining of spirituality than is our outreach in search of God. Von Balthasar writes 'Whatever could we say to God if he himself had not taken the first step in communicating and manifesting himself to us in his word, so that we have access to him and fellowship with him? ... The essential thing is for us to hear God's word and discover from it how to respond to him. His word is the truth, opened up to us ... God's word is his invitation to us to be with him in the truth ... God's word is himself, his most vital, his innermost self: his only-begotten Son, of the same nature as himself, sent into the world to bring it home, back to him.'[1]

And in this sense, we could go on to say, God is even more fundamentally 'I' than he is 'Thou'. He is antecedently 'I' because in his revelation as the Word he takes the initiative in finding us, rather than waiting to be found by us. In the words of Bouyer, 'He is this 'You' above all because He has manifested Himself to us as supremely the 'I', the One Who has not waited to meet us until we should take the first step, but Who has Himself taken the initiative in a dialogue between Him and ourselves'.[2]

The outreach is first of all corporate before it is individual, but that is not because it can ever lack an inter-personal character of some kind. In his corporate outreach to us, the divine 'I' addresses himself to the corporate 'theological persons'—to borrow a phrase from von Balthasar's theo-dramatics—that are in the

---

[1] von Balthasar, *Prayer*, p. 15.
[2] Bouyer, *Introduction to Spirituality*, p. 9.

first place Israel, and then the Church. That is not to exclude an intimate relation with each one of us. On the contrary, it is to make such intimate relations possible. It is within this corporate address that God's address to us as individual persons takes place. That means, then, that it will be in the Church that we shall find him. In the words of Louis Bouyer, again: 'by the express will of Christ' the Word is to be found 'only in His Body which is the Church' — an understandable enough state of affairs when we bear in mind that the Church is to be the instrument of that consummation of all things in Christ which is the goal of the divine saving plan.[3]

This connexion between the self-revealing Word and the Church explains why Scripture yields up the Word of God only when read in the Church's Tradition. The same Spirit who spoke through the prophetic voices of the Old Testament, animated the humanity of Christ in the New, and inspired the writers of the two Testaments to produce the biblical corpus, still assists the members of the Church to read the Bible correctly by the light he provides in Tradition. In *Dei Verbum*, the Dogmatic Constitution of the Second Vatican Council on Divine Revelation, we read, 'God who spoke of old uninterruptedly converses with the Bride of his beloved Son, and the Holy Spirit . . . leads into all truth those who believe and makes the word of God dwell abundantly in them'.[4]

The Word is found in the Church not only as the fact of the divine invitation to take part in an 'I–Thou' relationship but also as the truth of what that relationship will entail for us. The Word of God is not, in other words, an invitation that lacks a content. It is a

---

[3] *Ibid.*, p. 13.
[4] *Dei Verbum*, 2.

personal divine approach to us that brings along with it the truths we need for orienting ourselves in existence: truths about God, truths about man, truths about the world, and truths about the divine plan for bringing the world to its consummation. The approach to us of the divine Word is *content-filled*.

Spirituality and doctrine

That is why Christian spirituality, as a spirituality of the divine Word, is based on what has been called, in the context of the writings of the Swiss mystic Adrienne von Speyr, 'objective mysticism'.[5] Objective mysticism is the mysticism made possible when the divine Subject, in his approach to us, makes known, in the historic revelation carried by the Church, the full range of objective truth which we need for a spiritual life worthy of our human and Christian calling.[6]

Accordingly, we cannot have a spirituality without doctrine, just as we cannot have doctrine without Scripture read in Tradition: the primary witness to the Word that is Scripture, and the indispensable complementary witness that is Tradition. That does not mean that in spirituality we are called on to think systematically about the truth the Word brings. To suppose so would be to confuse spirituality with systematic

---

[5] Adrienne von Speyr, *Mistica oggettiva*, ed. Barbara Albrecht (Milan: Jaca Books, 1975).

[6] That the Church's dogma is necessary equipment for the journey to deification is the central thesis of Vladimir Lossky, *The Mystical Theology of the Eastern Church*. English trans. (London: James Clarke, 1957; reprinted Crestwood, NY: St Vladimir's Seminary Press, 1974).

theology. What we concentrate on in spirituality is how by means of the Word God seeks to enter my life.

To cohere with our doctrine, based as it is on the reception of the Word of God in divine revelation, spirituality must have five qualities in particular. It must be creation-founded, Trinitarian, Christological, Pneumatological and ecclesial. If human persons are to live with a life that really is in abiding relation to their Creator, the triune God, through Christ, by his Spirit, and all of this as mediated through the Church, this fivefold doctrinal character — creation-founded, Trinitarian, Christological, Pneumatological, ecclesial — is indispensable. It is the litmus test by which spirituality is found to be, as we say, 'orthodox'.

Those five adjectives need visiting in turn. First, orthodox spirituality is *creation-founded*. Only if there is both the distance and the closeness between God and ourselves that the Creator-creature relation implies can there be the union of love that Christian spirituality affirms as its own desired outcome. God is already intimately present to us by creation, but he is also, as Creator, enfolded in utter mystery, beyond not only everything in the world but beyond the world as a whole. He is distant and he is close, transcendent and immanent.

Moreover, both divine freedom and human freedom must be given their rightful due, so that God can be said to open himself gratuitously, freely, to invite human persons to share his life, and human persons can willingly choose to grow spiritually in response to the divine. Von Balthasar remarks of this further element in the creature-Creator relation, 'this fellowship of being ... can only persist if it is also at the level of spirit, i.e. if the Word's freedom is matched by a corresponding readiness on man's side to hear, follow and accept'.[7] What von Balthasar is saying is: the creature-Creator relation is not just a given. It is also a task. We do not simply exist in relation to God, the self-existent One. As human beings, we are free potential respondents in relation to the primordial freedom of God.

Secondly, orthodox spirituality is *Trinitarian*. To anticipate what will come later, the ascetical and mystical path turns on the 'purification' and 'illumination' of the person so that each one may by love be in 'union' with Love itself. This mutual abiding in love is the Word's ultimate New Testament promise, above all in the Gospel according to John and the Letters of St John. But to say that God is Love itself implies that the one God, our Creator, is not a solitary Monad. For God to be Love (and not just loving) there must be an eternal communion of loving relations in God. Only Trinitarian belief can sustain that entailment. And in any case, since Christian faith is 'specified in its entirety by Christ', it cannot be other than a Trinitarian faith since 'its object is Christ in whom we find the three Persons; its source is the grace of Christ, in whom the "Author of beatitude", the Triune God, gives and reveals himself'.[8] This brings us to the third of spirituality's doctrinal prerequisites.

Thirdly, then, orthodox spirituality is *Christological*. The Source of the Trinity, the Father, wanted to com-

---

[7] von Balthasar, *Prayer*, pp. 21–2.
[8] Jean Mouroux, *I Believe. The Personal Structure of Faith*. English trans. (Sheed and Ward: New York, 1960), p. 37. Mouroux devised the phrase 'author of beatitude' as an encapsulation of Aquinas's doctrine of faith. 'I tend towards God as First Truth because I tend to him as the source of beatitude ... there are no truths of faith except in relation to God as First Truth and to God as the author of beatitude', *ibid.*, p. 18. Cf. Thomas Aquinas, *Summa theologiae*, IIa. IIae., q. 1, a. 7.

municate his love to human creatures in paternal form, that is, in a way that corresponds to the Father's love for his Son. We had already been created in the image of the Son, but with the incarnation of the Word as Jesus Christ, the Father's love for the Son is extended to Christ's brethren, to human beings. As the Romanian theologian Dumitru Staniloae has it, combining a metaphor of his own with the terminology of the great patristic Councils: 'Jesus Christ is the bridge stretching from the Father to the realm of our humanity, by His one hypostasis which unites both the divine and human natures'.[9] Christ is the only Mediator (I Timothy 2:5), a statement that can also be put in the language of St John's Gospel where the Saviour calls himself the 'Way, the Truth and the Life' (John 14:6).

For the Cistercian spiritual theologian Thomas Merton, the reason why Jesus Christ is not just the *Way* to the Father but also the *Truth* about the Father is that 'all the revealed words of God are partial manifestations of the Word, who is the splendour of God's Truth', just as the Son is likewise the *Life* of the Father because (in Merton's words again) that life is 'contained in the revealed Word' in its totality and is 'communicated by it'.[10] Not surprisingly, then, in the Letter to the Ephesians St Paul finds it to be through the Son that we 'have access in one Spirit to the Father' (Ephesians 2:18).

Paul's mention of the Holy Spirit brings me, fourthly, to the *pneumatological* dimension, a dimension governed by the *Pneuma*, the Spirit. Orthodox spirituality

---

[9] Dumitru Staniloae, *Orthodox Spirituality. A Practical Guide for the Faithful and a Definitive Manual for the Scholar*. English trans. (South Canaan, PN: St Tikhon's Seminary Press, 2002), p. 56.
[10] Thomas Merton, *Bread in the Wilderness* (London: Hollis and Carter, 1954), pp. 63, 64.

must be properly pneumatological. The Holy Spirit is poured out upon the Son as man, and then in turn, at Pentecost, is himself poured out by the crucified and glorified Son onto his brothers and sisters in the new Israel, his Church. 'Caught up ... to the "right hand of the Father", the Son's transfigured humanity becomes involved in the eternal spiration of the Holy Spirit, and the immediate consequence of this is that the Spirit is poured out into Christ's mystical body on earth.'[11]

The gift of the Spirit enables us to enter the sphere of God's own intra-Trinitarian life—but we do so through what von Balthasar terms the 'door' that is formed by the wound in the Son's side, without which we should not have known how the life of God is 'the highest degree of self-giving'.[12] It is through the Spirit we are drawn into the mystery of divine sonship, becoming adopted sons and daughters of the all-loving Father.

So, finally, orthodox spirituality is *ecclesial*, which means in the first place that it is baptismal. The fifth-century writer Mark the Monk begins his treatise on Baptism by reminding the reader how the ascetical and mystical journey depends on baptismal regeneration. 'O man, who was baptized in Christ, work as much as you are able, and prepare yourself to receive the appearance of the One who lives within you.'[13] Christ lives within us through the mysteries (that is, the sacraments), of initiation. By the washing of Baptism, the anointing with chrism, and the feeding from the eucharistic table, Christ 'comes to us and dwells in us; He is united to us and grows into one with us. He stifles sin in us and infuses into us his own life and

---

[11] von Balthasar, *Prayer*, pp. 69–70.
[12] Ibid., p. 69.
[13] Mark the Monk, *On Baptism*, 1.

merit.'[14] Thus the fourteenth-century Byzantine lay theologian St Nicholas Cabasilas. The mysteries of Baptism, Confirmation, and Eucharist, considered as the means of Jesus Christ's indwelling, are, in Staniloae's words, 'the source of indispensable divine power for ascetical efforts and for the living of the mystical life with Christ'.[15] We shall look into this more fully in due course. Here it suffices to note how the sacramental dimension inevitably means an ecclesial dimension. To cite Staniloae again, 'Where Christ is through the mysteries, there is the Church full of the Spirit in Him', or in another formulation, 'only the Church imparts Christ, as His Body, by means of the mysteries'.[16] So the individual spiritual pilgrim has to draw stimulus and inspiration from the faith community that is Holy Church, and especially from those within it, whether alive or dead, who have spiritual illumination to offer.

This is the special theme of the sixth-century Syrian monk who took as his pseudonym the name of a Greek pupil of St Paul's, Dionysius the Areopagite. For Dionysius the whole Church, mirroring the angelic realm, is a 'hierarchy', but 'hierarchy' is never for him just a matter of rank. Rather is it concerned with the enabling of 'knowledge and activity', and specifically those sorts of knowledge and activity which tend to bring people closer to the divine likeness, to unite them with God.[17] In von Balthasar's simple words, 'It is the holy people which is the hearer of the word; the individual Christian, the praying person, only exists as a

[14] Nicholas Cabasilas, *The Life in Christ*, I.11.
[15] Staniloae, *Orthodox Spirituality*, p. 62.
[16] Ibid.
[17] Andrew Louth, *Denys the Areopagite* (London: Geoffrey Chapman, 1989), p. 38.

member of this people'.[18] Or as Staniloae prefers to put it: 'The spiritual ascent, even if it carries someone close to God in Heaven is an ascent within the Church, on the spiritual steps of the Church on earth, and on those of the Church in Heaven. There is no other ladder to God, except the one in the Church.'[19]

Conclusion

So spirituality must be rich in doctrine, doing justice to its main dimensions: creation, Trinity, Christology, Pneumatology, ecclesiology. The great Anglo-Catholic philosopher and theologian Eric Mascall wrote in his memoirs: 'Unless prayer has the great Christian truths to feed upon it is bound to become weak and straggly, and in the end to feed simply on itself and starve to death. This is all the more necessary at a time when few people have received in their childhood the basic Christian formation that once could be taken for granted.'[20]

---

[18] von Balthasar, *Prayer*, p. 87.
[19] Staniloae, *Orthodox Spirituality*, p. 67.
[20] E. L. Mascall, *Saraband* (Leominster: Gracewing, 1992), p. 204.

✢ 2 ✢

The Liturgy as the Context

I ENDED THE LAST CHAPTER by describing orthodox spirituality as essentially ecclesial in character. The living divine Word who is attested in the words of Scripture convokes a holy people. We need now to take a further step. This convocation is rightly defined first and foremost as a *worshipping assembly*. This means, then, that relation with the Word, the Source of spirituality, has a *liturgical context*.

The Word welcomed in liturgical celebration

We can see this already in the dispensation of the Synagogue—that is, in the life of ancient Israel. Louis Bouyer draws attention in this regard to three great moments recorded in the Old Testament.[1] We see the role of the worshipping assembly in the reception of the Word in the course of the very first major public act of redemption: namely, the Exodus Sinai event. At Mount Sinai, the divine Word, speaking through Moses, called the people to a sacred assembly, precisely in order that they might hear that Word in his initial twofold self-revelation in the wilderness: twofold, because he first reveals his name, as I AM, and then

---

[1] Bouyer, *Introduction to Spirituality*, pp. 28–31.

reveals his will, summed up in the Ten Words, the Ten Commandments. The people accepted that message about God's identity and will in the liturgy of sacrifice which sealed the Mosaic covenant—as chapter 24 of the Book of Exodus describes.

This first biblical example of the way liturgical worship forms an essential context for the receiving of the Word established something of a pattern. It recurs in the second chief event of this kind: the reconsecration of the people to the Lord by the Judaean king Josiah in chapter 23 of the Second Book of Kings. Here the solemn reading of Deuteronomy, whose name means 'the second presentation of the Law', was once again contextualized and confirmed by sacrificial worship.

The third and last great moment in the corporate public reception of the Word by Israel occurred when Ezra, returning with the exiles from Babylon to begin the process of reconstituting Israel in the Land, reconvoked the assembly by reading out the Scriptures, the witness to the Word, and leading the people not in sacrifice, which was impossible (for the Temple lay in ruins), but in a solemn thanksgiving for all the mighty deeds of God for Israel—as described in the Book of Nehemiah (8:1–18).

The lesson from these three Old Testament highpoints—the making of the Sinai covenant, the renewal of covenant life before the Exile under Josiah and once again after the Exile with Ezra—is that the Word of God is typically welcomed in liturgical celebration. This in turn looks ahead to the structure of the liturgy of the Church, the new Israel. Von Balthasar wrote: 'receptivity for the word of God constitutes the central act of the Church's liturgy, in which we can discern two phases: the reception of the Word as word [he means, as Scripture], and the reception of the Word as flesh [he means in the eucharistic sacrament],[2] the latter depending, of course, on the revelation to Israel reaching its climax in the incarnation of the Word as Jesus Christ.

The written Word in the liturgical context

The liturgy of the Great Church, Eastern and Western, makes use of the Pentateuch, the Prophets and the other 'writings' in which the Word of God witnessed to his own activity in Israel, and it adds to these the apostolic writings, above all the Gospels, which testify to the culmination of the Word's activity in the incarnation, death and resurrection of the Son of God.

By calling to mind in the liturgy the great events whereby God gradually revealed his saving plan, the Church echoes the divine pedagogy and enables us to locate the unity of revelation in its long, cumulative history in Jesus Christ. But because all this is in aid of God's outreach to us in inter-personal relations through his Word, it needs to be internalized, along the lines of St Paul's phrase in the Letter to the Colossians, 'Christ in you, the hope of glory' (Colossians 1:27).

To this end, the texts of the liturgy, in the way they present the Bible, provide us with *spiritual interpretation*. The spiritual interpretation of Scripture is a different matter from the historical interpretation found in the Academy, though it should not be understood over against the latter. Spiritual interpretation presupposes historical interpretation as its own indispensable basis. But spiritual exegesis as offered by the liturgy is the only kind which enables us to attain the plenary mean-

---

[2] von Balthasar, *Prayer*, p. 108.

ing of the Bible, necessary as this is for a full spiritual life. It is a form of biblical interpretation that takes sacred history to be prolonged through time so as to reach ourselves in whatever age we live, and indeed to extend beyond our own times into the indefinite future. That prolongation (or, as it is sometimes called, 'actualization') of the Bible is accessible only to faith. The faith to which it is accessible is, however, precisely the faith taught by the Scriptures themselves, since the Old Testament authors appeal to the redemptive acts of the past in order to throw light on the moral demands of the present, and they find in those acts figures or fore-shadowings of later eschatological realities. In the New Testament, furthermore, the sacred writers judge these earlier moments of divine self-revelation to be fulfilled Christologically, fulfilled, that is, in Jesus Christ. The Bible itself, then, lays the foundation of the kind of spiritual interpretation practised in the liturgy.[3]

The way in which it does so gives us the meanings the classic understanding of spiritual exegesis has schematized in the various 'senses' of Scripture it identifies. There are, basically, three of them — the moral (often called 'tropological'), the eschatological (often called 'anagogical') and the Christological (often called 'allegorical'). Spiritual exegesis consists in the sum of these three.

In a personal use of the spiritual exegesis performed by the liturgy we transpose the biblical text by applying it to ourselves individually as members of the Church. In *Bread in the Wilderness* Thomas Merton furnishes an excellent example. 'Just as the whole people of God is still crossing the desert to the Promised

---

[3] Jean Daniélou, *The Bible and the Liturgy* (Notre Dame, IN: University of Notre Dame Press, 1956).

Land, still passing through the Jordan, still building Jerusalem and raising God's temple on Sion, so each individual soul must normally know something of the same journey, the same hunger and thirst, the same battles and prayers, light and darkness, the same sacrifices and the same struggle to build Jerusalem within itself'.[4] We are to interiorize the message of Scripture, as in the moral or tropological sense. We are to live out its message in hope, as in the eschatological or anagogical sense. And we are to focus its message on Jesus Christ who is to become, by our participation in his life, our very own, as in the Christological or allegorical sense. Merton's text does not mention the last, but he is far from neglecting it, whether in the work cited or elsewhere.[5]

I have set out the three senses of Scripture in the order tropological, anagogical, allegorical. Bouyer prefers to order them in the sequence allegorical, tropological, anagogical, because he can show better how they fit together that way. As he writes: 'The allegorical sense of St Paul and the Fathers means that in Christ is definitively realized everything that foreshadowed Him in ascending towards Him and preparing us for Him. This meaning is transferred to us by the tropological sense, which is not simply any kind of moral application of Scripture to each of us, but that very defi-

---

[4] Merton, *Bread in the Wilderness*, p. 83.
[5] Numerous texts are collated in John J. Higgins, SJ, *Merton's Theology of Prayer* (Spencer, MA: Cistercian Publications, 1971), pp. 11–24, a study which takes as its epigram a statement Merton made in an address of 10 November 1963: 'Whatever I may have written, I think it all can be reduced in the end to this one root truth: that God calls human persons to union with Himself and with one another in Christ, in the Church which is His Mystical Body', cited, this time with its source, *ibid.*, p. xiv.

nite application resulting from our faith in the life of Christ in us. And, in turn, this tropological meaning, by virtue of the perspectives it opens out to our hope—of the fullness of Christ becoming our fullness—finds its final flowering in anagogy, the anticipated attainment of the eschatological realities.'[6] In other words, to put the senses of Scripture in the order allegorical—tropological—anagogical, allows the spiritual theologian to explain more readily how all three are ultimately about the mystery of Christ, the mystery we are to enter and share.

Disengaging a further implication of the last of the three (in his ranking), namely, the anagogical or eschatological meaning of Scripture, Bouyer adds a further remark important for any discussion of the mystical 'outcome' of spirituality: 'this anagogical sense becomes—in the final meaning given to the term by the Fathers, the mystical sense of Scripture—the meaning which causes us to discover to the degree which is possible here below, the experience by anticipation of everlasting life.'[7] Such spiritual understanding of Scripture is not just another interpretative tool. It is a spiritual exercise that, in the words of Merton, summarizing here the teaching of the fifth-century Church father St John Cassian, 'goes hand in hand with purity of heart and true contemplation'.[8]

In the New Covenant, the liturgical context of spirituality is closely connected with the fullest possible expression of the Word of God, which surpasses the Old Covenant in what St Paul terms *mysterion*: 'the

---

[6] Bouyer, *Introduction to Spirituality*, p. 38.
[7] *Ibid.*, p. 39.
[8] Merton, *Bread in the Wilderness*, p. 17, with reference to St John Cassian, *Conferences*, XIV.

mystery'. By 'the mystery' Paul means the revelation of divine wisdom in the plan of God to reconcile all human beings in Christ (the emphasis in his Letter to the Colossians) and, more cosmically, to recapitulate or gather together all things in him (the emphasis in his Letter to the Ephesians). This is the mystery accomplished in the great redemptive act of the death of Christ and its consequences in the Resurrection and the sending of the Spirit. The Mass is the principal liturgical expression of this mystery, which also, however, finds a manifestation in the other sacraments and in the Divine Office (the liturgy of the Hours) as the Church year unfolds.

That the Mass is the liturgical expression of the triumphant sacrificial death of the Word incarnate has been the common teaching of Catholic theologians since at least the Council of Trent.[9] That the other sacraments bear an essential relation to the Mass, has been the conviction of many major theologians, including St Thomas.[10] That other liturgical media, notably the liturgy of the Hours and the cycle of feast and fast in the Church year, also communicate the mystery of Christ, was the insight of the great twentieth-century German theologian of the liturgy Dom Odo Casel, a monk of the Rhineland abbey of Maria Laach, who explains it in his book *The Mystery of Christian Worship*.[11]

[9] A case is made for its priority in organizing the motifs of this sacrament in Aidan Nichols, OP, 'The Holy Oblation: On the Primacy of Eucharistic Sacrifice', *Downside Review* 122.429 (2004), pp. 259–72.

[10] Aidan Nichols, 'St Thomas and the Sacramental Liturgy', *The Thomist* 72 (2008), pp. 1–23, reprinted in his *Lost in Wonder. Essays on Liturgy and the Arts* (Aldershot: Ashgate, 2011), pp. 3–20.

[11] Odo Casel, OSB, *The Mystery of Christian Worship*. English trans. (New York: Crossroad, 1999).

Participation in the liturgy of the Church as a whole must be understood from the vantage point of 'the mystery'. The Orthodox patristic scholar Andrew Louth draws attention to the derivation of our word 'mystical' from the mystery so conceived, and how in the vocabulary of Tradition the term has branched out to express the scriptural, liturgical and personal dimensions of that supreme *Mysterion*. 'In Christian vocabulary *mystikos* means something that refers us to this mystery of God's love for us in Christ and makes it accessible to us.'[12]

'The mystery', then, is not simply a disclosure of a divine design. God reveals not just his working plan, he reveals *himself*. He puts himself into his work. The Word—and the mystery is the highpoint of the revelation of the Word—brings not only a message, some information to add to what we know from a rational metaphysics. The Word brings the very life of the triune God, impacting the world for its salvation, above all, through the mysteries of Christ's life, death and exaltation—the last of which includes Pentecost, and Parousia. By their causal efficacy the mysteries of Christ bring about the regeneration, sanctification and ultimately the resurrection of the redeemed, and by their exemplary causality they shape the existence of Christ's disciples on the model of his own.[13] It is the task of the liturgy of the Church to bring all this home to the baptized.

---

[12] Louth, *Denys the Areopagite*, p. 28.
[13] See Aidan Nichols, OP, *Deep Mysteries. God, Christ and Ourselves* (Lanham, MD: Lexington Books, 2018).

Spirituality and the sacramental life

The liturgy is more than the sacraments, as the 1992 *Catechism of the Catholic Church* explains in its second book. But the sacraments enjoy a uniquely efficacious power to apply to us the mystery as centred on the humanized Trinitarian Son, Jesus Christ, in his death, Resurrection, and sending of the Spirit. They are, in the term the Greek Fathers used in their sacramental commentaries, 'mystagogical' events. The sacraments, celebrated liturgically, lead us into the mystery.[14]

Mystagogically speaking, Baptism, Chrismation (or Confirmation), and the Holy Eucharist are the most important of the sacraments. Indeed, Nicholas Cabasilas, in his treatise *The Life in Christ*, a study of the sacramental life mentioned in the previous chapter, confines himself to comment on these three.

Baptism comes first. Supporting, from a combination of biblical, patristic and scholastic sources, the idea of a call of all Christians to mystical union with God, Dom Anselm Stolz, a monk of Gerleve (in Westphalia), wrote: 'Every Christian, so far as he shares in the redemptive work of Christ, is undoubtedly invited to a restoration of the lost grace of Paradise and to the vision of God. In the grace of redemption bestowed upon him by the sacrament of Baptism, a man must be granted the capacity for attaining to the highest mystical union, since mystical union and the full evolution of

---

[14] Mazza demonstrates this by reference to the patristic authors of 'mystagogical catecheses': Enrico Mazza, *Mystagogy. A Theology of the Liturgy in the Patristic Age*. English trans. (New York: Pueblo, 1989). See too for this foundation of all Christian life Alexander Schmemann, *Of Water and the Spirit* (Crestwood, NY: St Vladimir's Seminary Press, 1974).

justifying grace mean the same thing.'[15] Andrew Louth, having considered the writers of the Platonist school (whether pagan or Jewish) who established much of the language of the mystical theologians of the Christian tradition, flags up a radical difference between any of these pre-Christian or non-Christian thinkers on the one hand and, on the other, the divines of the ancient Church. Only the latter—for obvious reasons—can do justice to the essential role of Christian Baptism in the spiritual life. 'The ascent begins, or is made possible, by what God has done for us in Christ and made effective in us by baptism. The mystical life is the working-out, the realizing, of Christ's union with the soul effected in Baptism, and is a communion, a dialogue between Christ and the soul.'[16] In Baptism, the first of the sacraments on any listing, we are conformed to Christ dead and risen, introduced into the royal priesthood of the holy people of God, and fitted to share in the liturgy at its high-point, the Holy Eucharist. Initiation into Christianity is engrafting into Christ, and both initiation and engrafting require entry into the Church, the climax of which is participation in the Holy Eucharist. That is why baptism ideally takes place at the Easter Vigil, when the heart of the Christian mystery is celebrated eucharistically. In the baptismal waters Christian initiates themselves ritually die and rise again, dying as in the Flood-waters that made an end of a corrupted world, rising as in the living or maternal water over which the Holy Spirit broods so that new life may come (compare the opening words of the Book of Genesis).

---

[15] Anselm Stolz, OSB, *The Doctrine of Spiritual Perfection*. English trans. (St Louis, MO: Herder, 1938), p. 32.
[16] Andrew Louth, *The Origins of the Christian Mystical Tradition* (Oxford: Clarendon, 1983), p. 53.

St Paul has a wealth of images for the new life in Christ which results. Christians have become one plant (one 'olive-tree') with Christ, so the Letter to the Romans (11:17). As with their own clothing they have 'put on' Christ: thus the Letter to the Galatians (3:27). They are members of Christ's Body: thus the First Letter to the Corinthians (12:12–30). More generally, in the Pauline letters there is a plethora of *syn*-words, words that indicate a being 'together with Christ' since, through Baptism, the life of Christians is 'with' his life, being one with him as the New Adam.

Confirmation, the sacrament of the chrism, is described in ancient texts as the 'seal' of Baptism. It sinks more deeply into us the presence and action of the Holy Spirit. 'You have received the Spirit of adopted sons which makes you cry out, 'Abba, Father'. The Spirit in person joins himself to our spirit to attest that we are children of God (Romans 8:16–17). This set of affirmations Paul repeats almost word for word in the Letter to the Galatians (4:6–7). The Spirit teaches us to 'pray as we ought', is the teaching of Paul in the Letter to the Romans (8:26), and, according to the Letter to the Ephesians, the Spirit also gives us *parrhesia*: namely, the freedom to speak out boldly (3:12, 6:19). Dumitru Staniloae wrote of the gifts of the Spirit received in Chrismation: 'Strictly speaking, in distinction to the grace of Baptism which directs the work of mortifying the old man and of the general growth of the new, they [the Spirit's gifts in the chrisma] are intended to remake and intensify the powers of the knowledge of the soul and of courageous perseverance in God ... They are first of all ... gifts for enlightening the mind [compare St Paul's 'pray as we ought'], and, precisely because of this, gifts for its fortification in its orientation towards God [compare St Paul's *parrhesia*, to speak out boldly]. Therefore they show their full efficiency only when our intellectual powers, which work with them, have been sufficiently developed.'[17] Being chrismated, receiving the sacrament of Confirmation, as a pre-adult, or indeed, in the Byzantine rite, as an infant, will inevitably, then, be delayed in its proper effect. That does not make the sacramental act any less real. Cabasilas wrote in *The Life in Christ*: 'Of the various rites each has its own effect; participation of the Spirit and of His gifts depends on the most holy chrism. Therefore, while one may not be able to demonstrate the spiritual gift at the very time that the sacred rite takes place, but only much later, we should not be ignorant of the cause and origin of the power.'[18] Of course many Christians never become fully aware of the spiritual treasure they have received through Chrismation. In his treatise, Cabasilas has already pointed out that not all have the perception of the gifts or the eagerness to use the riches they have been given.

After discussion of Baptism and Chrismation seems a suitable juncture at which to insert some reference to the sacrament of *Penance* or Confession, which in modern Catholic parlance is often called the 'sacrament of Reconciliation' and in Orthodox theology the 'sacrament of Repentance'. The reason for so doing is that this sacrament re-establishes Christians in the privileges of initiation, i.e. in the privileges of, precisely, Baptism and Confirmation. In ancient Christianity that was made apparent on Holy Thursday when the bishop would go to the porch seeking out the Church's penitents so as to reconcile them in good time for them

---

[17] Staniloae, *Orthodox Spirituality*, p. 195.
[18] Cabasilas, *The Life in Christ*, III. 6.

to take part in the Paschal celebration, when Baptism and Chrismation would be conferred on pagans, which Christian penitents once were.

More particularly, the sacrament of Penance brings out the meaning of the exorcism and the anointing with the oil of catechumens that form part of the rite of Baptism. These prayers and gestures are essentially concerned with holy warfare, which the penitent Christian will have experienced in the struggle of the moral life. 'In the present economy of sin repaired by the cross, the Spirit of God takes possession of our spirit only through a victorious struggle with the spirit of evil.'[19] At Baptism, the Cross of Christ is signed on Christians, as the crucified Lord makes them his own. United with Christ, and filled with his Spirit they are then to continue that struggle. The rites of Baptism include the renunciation of Satan and the affirmation of adherence to Christ, and these are renewed in personal living through continuing repentance, an ongoing conversion of which not just the sacrament of Penance but (more widely) the development of the virtue of penitence form an integral part.

In Bouyer's account of the inter-relation between spirituality and the sacramental life, not only the sacrament of Penance but also the sacraments of *Orders, Marriage and Anointing of the Sick* are discussed prior to the sacrament of the Holy Eucharist.[20] This of course has the disadvantage of appearing to separate the Eucharist from the other sacraments of initiation. But by leaving the Eucharist until last it can, he thinks, the better serve as a suitable climax to all seven.

---

[19] Bouyer, *Introduction to Spirituality*, p. 117.
[20] Ibid., pp. 117–21.

The sacrament of *Holy Order*, bringing into existence as it does a distinct body—the ordained ministers—within the Church organism, raises the question of a possible differentiation of spirituality as between different groupings in the Church, an issue to which, notably in its ascetic aspect, I shall return. More to the point, when discussing the liturgy as context, is what Bouyer has to say about *Matrimony and the Anointing of the Sick*. These are paired by him, an unusual procedure, for the sacraments of Marriage and the Anointing of the Sick seem an ill-assorted duo. But they do have something in common. Both are concerned with the restoring of creation. Matrimony takes the sacrificial love of the Cross into the biological and psychological realms of fertility and intimacy, and the Anointing of the Sick strengthens human weakness in those who are ill, with a view to ending physical and psychological suffering by the power of Christ—if not now then at any rate in the Resurrection, in the Age to Come, when there will be a transformed biology, already heralded in this sacrament.

Taken together, therefore, Matrimony and the Anointing of the Sick draw attention to creation-restoring dimensions of the sacramental life, Matrimony now, and Anointing either now or in the Age to Come, and if they do that for the sacramental life then they do it also for the spiritual life the context of which—so I am suggesting—the sacramental liturgy forms. Cosmic and eschatological dimensions thus show up on the radar screen as inherent features of the spiritual world to which asceticism and mysticism belong.

These cosmic and eschatological dimensions should not be regarded, however, as confined to the two sacraments just mentioned. The Russian Orthodox theologian of the liturgy Alexander Schmemann wrote: 'A sacrament [he means 'any sacrament'] is both cosmic and eschatological. It refers at the same time to God's world as he first created it and to its fulfillment in the kingdom of God. It is cosmic in that it embraces all of creation, it returns it to God as God's own ... and in and by itself it manifests the victory of Christ. But it is to the same degree eschatological, oriented towards the *kingdom which is to come*. For, having rejected and killed Christ—its Creator, Saviour and Lord—'this world' sentenced itself to death, as it does not have 'life in itself' and rejected him of whom it was said, 'In his was life and this life was the light of men' (John 1:14) ... thus those who believe in Christ and accept him as the "Way, the Truth and the Life" live in hope of the age to come. But this is precisely the joy of Christianity, the paschal essence of its faith.'[21] Schmemann ends his comments on sacraments as cosmic and eschatological by referring, then, to the Paschal mystery of Resurrection through the Cross, and this returns us to the Church's supreme expression and act, the Holy Eucharist.

The *Eucharist*, the third and last of the sacraments of initiation, is also the supreme sacrament of the seven. In the Eucharist, Christ is present as the glorious victim, sacrificed on the Cross, triumphant in heaven. The Cross is made present as our way to the Father in which, by the sacramental sacrifice, we can be united with the mediator in his crucial act of redemption which constitutes our hope of glory. 'Thus the Eucharist, as the perfect fulfilment of baptism, is the proper sacrament of mysticism', a claim which Stolz, the German Catholic monk, defends by reference to

---

[21] Alexander Schmemann, *The Eucharist, Sacrament of the Kingdom* (Crestwood, NY: St Vladimir's Seminary Press, 1988), pp. 34–5.

the *Life in Christ* of Cabasilas, the Byzantine Orthodox layman.[22] The Cross is made eucharistically present specifically as opening out onto the Resurrection and Ascension, the sending of the Spirit and the ultimate glorious Parousia of the end of the ages. In Alexander Schmemann's glowing words, 'The Church ... fulfils in the eucharist her ascension and entrance into the light and joy and triumph of the kingdom'.[23]

Like all the sacraments, the Holy Eucharist is a sign of these realities that effects what the sign signifies — if the participants permit it. 'If the participants permit it': this names a key condition. In a saying of von Balthasar's, 'The Eucharist demands contemplation'.[24] Without truly prayerful participation it cannot achieve its spiritual purpose. For Andrew Louth, *The Mystical Theology*—another influential treatise by Dionysius the Areopagite—is centrally concerned with 'the heart of the [eucharistic] liturgy' or as he puts it, the 'inner "mystic" meaning' of the Liturgy, rather than, as has commonly been assumed in the West, a recipe for the private prayer of individuals.[25] 'The liturgical action is an invitation to open oneself to the divine love: to respond to that invitation is to allow the whole of one's life to be transformed, to be deified, to become a vehicle for God's love in the world.'[26] This will be to understand the *Mystical Theology* in the context of Dionysius's twin treatises on how the divine is mediated via 'celestial' and 'ecclesiastical' hierarchies—the titles he

---

[22] Stolz, *The Doctrine of Spiritual Perfection*, p. 50. See further on 'eucharistic mysticism' William Johnston, *Christian Mysticism Today* (London: Collins, 1984), pp. 94–115.
[23] Schmemann, *The Eucharist, Sacrament of the Kingdom*, p. 43.
[24] von Balthasar, *Prayer*, p. 27.
[25] Louth, *Denys the Areopagite*, p. 108.
[26] Ibid.

gives to his writings about the angels on the one hand, the Church and the liturgy on the other.

And why not? The liturgical context of spirituality is meant indeed to affect all our prayer. An 'aliturgical prayer' which lacks connexion with the liturgy is dangerously under-exposed to the 'sense of the Church', the Church's own deepest mind-set which, thanks to her guidance by the Holy Spirit, will always be found to correspond to the meaning of the Word, the meaning God wants to convey to the world. 'Continually referring to the sense of the Church helps ... a person better than anything else to distinguish what is authentically 'spiritual' in himself from what is fallacious, and thus strengthens him and assures his further progress in the ways of the Spirit. Thus—by continually going back and forth between the prayer which is most personal, least reducible to any formula however excellent, and one which makes use of the most sober and pure formulae of the living tradition of the people of God is true prayer woven, the prayer of the Christian who in one movement becomes more fully the child of God in becoming always more fully the child of the Church'.[27]

The role of the communion of saints

Finally, then, on the topic of the liturgical context of spirituality, we can note that the liturgy is celebrated within the communion of the angels and saints.

Certain aids in the spiritual life derive from this connexion: reading lives of the saints; going on pilgrimage to holy places where the saints themselves have prayed; venerating the images or relics of the saints

---

[27] Bouyer, *Introduction to Spirituality*, p. 45.

which express in some way 'the invisible presence of ... those who are already perfect in their participation in [the Saviour's] mysteries'.[28] Speaking of the place of prayer to the saints in the spiritual life, the Greek theologian Giorgios Mantzarides has this to say:

> Seeking their [the saints'] intercession, we do not seek new mediators. There is one God and mediator, Christ. But when we seek the intercession of the saints, we show our humility and unworthiness, and we beseech God to give us his mercy, not because we are worthy of it, but for the sake of the saints who belong to the body of Christ, in which we also have been included and where we wish to remain in order to be saved.[29]

The communion of saints is hardly thinkable without developing a habit of asking the intercession of the saints themselves, above all of the Mother of God, the eschatological image of the perfection to which the whole Church is to tend. It also involves associating ourselves with the angels in their ceaseless contemplation, and with the dead in Christ 'whom our intercession accompanies to the end of their purification, just as theirs precedes us to the presence of the Father'.[30] Recourse to spiritual masters, for edification and inspiration in the Christian life, belongs here as well.[31] These practices flesh out the claim that in the

---

[28] Ibid., p. 309.
[29] Giorgios L. Mantzarides, *Orthodox Spiritual Life*. English trans. (Brookline, MA: Holy Cross Orthodox Press, 1994), p. 98.
[30] Bouyer, *Introduction to Spirituality*, p. 310.
[31] For a spirituality expressed via the favourite themes of eight such 'masters' from the twentieth century (six Catholic, one Orthodox, one Anglican), see Aidan Nichols, OP, *A Spirituality for the Twenty-First Century* (Huntington, IN: Our Sunday Visitor, 2003). That work was an orchestration of some spiritual

liturgy the Church is, in Schmemann's words, the 'sacrament of the Kingdom'. It is the context where the Word issues his invitation—an invitation to holiness.

themes for the Church in choir-stall and city, and not, like the present study, a presentation of a spiritual theology for each member of the faithful personally.

✢ 3 ✢

Meditation and Contemplation

THE STARTING-POINT OF MEDITATION and contemplation for the ancient Church, especially in the West, is surely *lectio divina*, or what came to be called 'spiritual reading'.

Lectio in its liturgical background

Here again, as with the source of spirituality in the Bible, and the context of spirituality in the liturgy, the Word of God, destined to have its maximal expression in 'The mystery', is to be the permanent centre of attention. All spiritual reading should have at its heart the understanding of the Word, witnessed to by Scripture especially as the Bible is appropriated by the Church in the setting of her liturgy. That does not mean that all prayer must necessarily begin by recalling Scripture in a verbal way. Yet, so Louis Bouyer maintains, 'prayer will be truly Christian only to the extent to which it is fed from the living store left in our memory by the divine Word, previously read or heard'.[1]

Lectio divina is the main way in which the texts of the liturgy—and, above all, the Scriptures, primary as these are in the words spoken at the Mass and in the

---

[1] Bouyer, *Introduction to Spirituality*, p. 46.

Divine Office—can be extended into our interior life. There are various ways of approaching its practice. One is by a complete reading of Scripture, book by book but in small, manageable sections, perhaps once a year. Another is to take a given book within Scripture and read it in its entirety. These two methods share a name, 'continuous reading' or, in Latin, *lectio continua*. Either of them is best practised when tutored by the liturgical tradition. Bouyer lays out a helpful scheme for this though ordinary Latin Catholics should note the date of his writing—on the eve of the Second Vatican Council and thus before the promulgation of the revised General Calendar of the Roman rite by Pope Paul VI in 1969.

Bouyer proposes the pre-Lenten season—the two and a half weeks of Septuagesima, Sexagesima, Quinquagesima, a time of preparation for re-living the mystery of redemption—as a suitable part of the Church year for reading the Book of Genesis. It is an appropriate time in which to refresh our sense of creation, the Fall, the foreshadowing of judgment and salvation in the story of Noah, and then the first appearance of the holy People of God in Abraham and the other patriarchs, who are 'our fathers in the faith'.[2] These are the great topics of the Book of Genesis.

The Book of Exodus fits well with Lent itself, because the Lenten season is a time to ponder the wilderness wandering and the entry into the Promised Land. For Passiontide, there might appropriately be Jeremiah, and the Servant Songs of Isaiah[3]—as well

---

[2] *Ibid.*, p. 49.
[3] On this see John F. A. Sawyer, *The Fifth Gospel. Isaiah in the History of Christianity* (Cambridge: Cambridge University Press, 1996).

as, obviously enough, the Passion narratives of all four Gospels, usefully complemented as these are by the commentary on the Paschal mystery that is the Letter to the Hebrews.

Suitable *lectio* material for Eastertide will include the Acts of the Apostles, 'the first steps of the Church in the light of the resurrection and Pentecost',[4] as well as the Letters of St Peter and St John, and the Letter of St James. The time after Pentecost fits well with the historical books, the sapiential books, and those prophetic books not already mentioned, though the Book of Isaiah in its entirety is best kept for Advent and Christmastide. The Pauline epistles, considered as classic explications of the Christian mystery, might be reserved for Epiphany and the weeks immediately following. The Gospels should never be marginal in *lectio* at any season, but the baptismal and eucharistic overtones of the early chapters of St John make them well suited to the end of Lent, while the chapters that run from the raising of Lazarus to the Farewell Discourse, with their teaching on the Lord's going to the Father and sending of the Paraclete, fit nicely into Eastertide.

These recommendations follow the calendar of St John XXIII, but they can be adapted to the calendar of Blessed Paul VI where the two differ. The only substantial difference concerns pre-Lent, which disappeared in the revision of the Western rite. By way of exception, the calendar of the newly created ordinariates for former Anglicans retains this ancient season, following here the calendar of John XXIII. For the rest, Bouyer's proposals fit admirably the new Roman Lectionary for the Proper of Seasons—on whose composition, as a member of the *consilium* appointed to execute

---

[4] Bouyer, *Introduction to Spirituality*, p. 49.

the liturgical reform desired by the Second Vatican Council, he presumably had his say.

Lectio can be expected to be fruitful in proportion to the spiritual culture of the person doing the reading—and the aforesaid means of reading or studying Scripture are relevant to the building up of a personal spiritual culture based on Bible and liturgy, and hence they are desirable if not absolutely necessary for the practice of *lectio*. But we have not yet embarked on the question of *lectio divina* in the strict and proper sense of that phrase, because we have not yet asked, how in *lectio* do we actually *read*?

Lectio in itself

Lectio is unlike the reading we do normally. For one thing, the text we ponder should be brief, the time we give it long. Also, in normal circumstances we read *in order to have read*. But here we read *in order to read*. It might help a little if we put ourselves back into the mindset of Christians in the ancient world who, like everyone else in late Antiquity, found books an expensive rarity. The form of the text, where for the sake of saving space words followed each other without gaps on the parchment, made reading a more demanding process than it is with us, and thus a much slower process—very usefully, for the purposes of *lectio divina* which cannot be hurried. 'Speed-reading', in the words of Dom David Foster of Downside, is 'the absolute enemy of *lectio divina*.'[5] In the ancient world reading was usually done with accompanying vocalization,

---

[5] David Foster, OSB, *Reading with God. Lectio Divina* (London: Continuum, 2005), p. 16.

however quiet. St Augustine mentions how struck he was at his first encounters with St Ambrose that when Ambrose was engaged in solitary reading there seemed to be no sound.[6] Vocalization, normal even when reading in solitude, helped to rub in the meaning of what one was reading—far more so than is the case nowadays when we merely run our eye along and down a printed page.

Most importantly, the reading done in *lectio* is motivated by a conviction about sacrality. As Christians we hold that the biblical text *contains* the Word of God (or, if it be a liturgical text or spiritual classic we are reading in *lectio*, this liturgical or spiritual text *is an echo or continuation of* the Word of God). It therefore needs to be attended to with the maximum care. Through these words as approached in the spirit of *lectio*, God himself seeks to speak to us.

If the Word is addressing himself to us now, it follows that we are to attend with all we are, with everything in us, with our problems as well as our delights. Everything about us should be brought to the reading, which explains the insistence of the ancient ascetical writers that here the mind must descend into the heart, the intelligence must reach down to the essential core of the entire personality. Typically, a biblical text will in some way or other both bid me do something and promise me some blessing, some reward. It will contain, either explicitly or implicitly, correlative commands and promises. The promises encourage us to pursue the commands, while the commands open out onto the promises which reward their performance. So I must be alert to what the Word bids me do, and attuned to the reward it may anticipate for

---

[6] Augustine, *Confessions*, VI. 3.

me. '*Lectio divina* is an "active" kind of reading in this sense: we are not just passive listeners to what God has said and done in the past. The words are addressed to us, and we are expected to do something. They are one side of a conversation, to which our prayer and lives are the response.'[7]

Prayer, vocal and mental

However, in and of itself *lectio* is not exactly prayer. For the mediaevals, *lectio* and *meditatio* led to *oratio* (and *contemplatio*) but they were not the same thing as that to which they aspired. Prayer requires acts of adoration, contrition, thanksgiving, supplication for myself or others. These are the chief modes of prayer as found in Scripture and at the liturgy, so they naturally take pride of place in personal prayer as well. (Incidentally the word 'acts' makes a useful mnemonic for remembering that list: 'a' for adoration, 'c' for contrition, 't' for thanksgiving, 's' for supplication.) By contrast, *lectio*, though it is of course meditative, can in principle proceed without any of these.

For this reason the English Benedictine monk-historian David Knowles considered *lectio*-meditation — or indeed any sort of meditation — to be 'strictly speaking ... not prayer at all'.[8] Rather, so he maintained, meditation is 'a preparation, a disposition, for prayer'.[9] Since, he went on, meditation is not yet prayer of any kind, there is not much point in going out of one's way (though it

---

[7] Foster, *Reading with God*, p. 1.
[8] David Knowles, *What is Mysticism?* (London: Burns and Oates, 1967), p. 66.
[9] *Ibid.*, p. 67.

is often done)to compare meditation and contemplation: to compare, that is, meditation and contemplative prayer. What, however, for Knowles does seem genuinely worthwhile is comparing with contemplation the kind of prayer into which 'words, thoughts and active impulses of the will enter as the constituent element'.[10] This is the kind of prayer typically exercised in the four modes already mentioned: adoration, contrition, thanksgiving and supplication. Here a comparison with contemplative prayer is perfectly feasible.

By contrast with such active prayer, wrote Knowles in pursuit of the comparison in question, 'pure contemplative prayer' is 'formless, infused love and knowledge; if it overflows into the normal faculties of the soul the words and feelings are its consequence, [they are] not itself'.[11] Unlike our ordinary active prayer, infused contemplation finds nothing easier than to dispense with words. It generates words, if at all, only as a side-effect. Most prayer cannot do this and should not be made to try.

Short of the wordless prayer of pure contemplation, prayer always uses words. The words it uses may be voiced externally or they may be formed interiorly. This distinction—external words or internal words—does not affect the status of our prayer. The contrasting of external and internal prayer, vocal prayer and mental prayer, is a post-patristic development of a rather unhelpful kind. Earlier, the relation between the two was seen as reciprocal, symbiotic. Interior prayer naturally expressed itself in vocal prayer, while such vocal prayer as the recitation of the psalms was expected to give interior prayer greater depth.

---

[10] *Ibid.*, p. 66.
[11] *Ibid.*

It would, then, be a mistake to think of these two kinds of prayer—interior prayer, exterior prayer—as heterogeneous. The recitation of the Divine Office, say, should not be considered a quite different sort of activity from anything involved in personal prayer. The example is a telling one, since, in point of fact, the pattern of the Divine Office lends itself well to prompting personal prayer, and especially, perhaps, the prayer of praise. Thus in the Western rite the offices of Lauds and Vespers sanctify, respectively, morning and evening by an offering of praise for God's work in creation (especially in the morning) and redemption (especially in the evening). In older Roman liturgical usage, the three psalms of praise which end the Psalter figure every day at Lauds, while other psalms of praise occur at Vespers. Although a morning call on God for help in the day ahead makes perfect sense, as does confession of faults and placing oneself in God's hands at the close of day, these themes of petition and contrition which became dominant in prayer manuals in the modern period have always been, in the official prayer of the Church in both East and West, subsidiary to praise for my creation and redemption.

The 'Little' Hours of Terce, Sext and None are not so little if we bear in mind their importance to the spiritual writers of the patristic centuries, who remark on the importance of this threefold turning to God in the middle of the morning's work, at noon-time, and as the night begins to set in. Prime, the first 'Day Hour' (surviving now only in the *Vetus Ordo* or older form of the Roman liturgy), and Compline, the last hour before retiring, are offices for the beginning of the day's work and the beginning of the night's sleep, and have psalmody that suits those occasions.

There remains in a survey of the vocal prayer of the office Matins or the Vigil service, which, as developed by monks, was dominated by the meditative reading of Scripture. Here the 'historical' psalms, which rehearse the *magnalia Dei* in saving history, and the 'sapiential' psalms, which delight in the thought of the Wisdom of God, have been especially favoured. Breaking one's sleep for prayer is something that can be done with profit by non-monastics as well. The middle of the night or the early hours of the morning are a tranquil time yet also a time when the thought of God may be furthest away.

The point of this apparent digression on the liturgy of the Hours is that for every Christian the divine Office, so far from being irrelevant to personal prayer, can usually provide an 'outline' of a prayer scheme that can accompany and penetrate daily life.[12] The Little Office of the Blessed Virgin Mary, once recited by many laypeople, especially tertiary members of religious orders, is a good example of a realistic scheme of vocal prayer, using the model of the Great Office, yet suited to busy people, or to those who may find it distracting to search about a complex Breviary in search of the correct texts. An excellent amplified version, following the pattern of the revised liturgy of the Hours, was published in 1988 with an imprimatur from the archdiocese of New York.[13] The wider conclusion is that vocal prayer—as in the liturgy of the Hours—can and should feed mental prayer, just as the texts it uses can be revisited time and again in the meditative form of *lectio divina*.

---

[12] Bouyer, *Introduction to Spirituality*, p. 68.
[13] John E. Rotelle, OSA (ed.), *Little Office of the Blessed Virgin Mary* (New Jersey: Catholic Book Publishing Corporation, 1988).

Meditation and contemplation

Meditation, whether or not prompted by *lectio*, has always been seen—so much even Knowles concedes—as a preparation or disposition for prayer, and if for prayer then also, ultimately—but this Knowles does *not* concede—for contemplative prayer.

On a once widespread view still normative in the Christian East (but, under post-Renaissance Western influence, not shared by some Latins), contemplation is the deep outflow of prayer as such. When, especially in the sixteenth century, methods of meditation became systematized in the Western tradition, the idea arose that meditation and contemplation were not only essentially different. More than that, they were quite separate affairs. Indeed, in a certain perspective they could even be regarded as opposed to each other. And this is the perspective Knowles adopts.

Expressed for the first time in the writings of Teresa of Avila, the perspective in question contrasts *activity* on the one hand with *passivity* on the other. Meditation is an *activity*, initiated by human beings who, however—let it be said—are already in receipt of the gift of faith from God. Were that not so, theirs would hardly be specifically *Christian* meditative activity. By contrast, contemplation is a *passivity*, a mode of prayer initiated not by human beings—who simply undergo it—but directly by God. Since the origination of this kind of Christian prayer belongs to a sub-set of gracious divine actions, it must be termed extra-ordinary in character. In his provident selection of extraordinary graces, God bestows the gift of specifically contemplative prayer on specially chosen souls. The sign that this is happening, so the Carmelite doctors—Teresa and John of the

Cross typically report, will be the inability of such rare individuals to continue with formal meditation.

On the Carmelite understanding, facility in meditation is acquired by long and diligent practice, as with any good habit. By contrast, contemplation is not acquired as good habits are acquired, namely by those who are faithful in repeatedly carrying out the acts that belong to the habit in question. Instead, contemplation is sheerly infused, as the theological virtues of faith, hope and charity are sheerly infused by supernatural divine agency. No amount of practice can induce infusion. Infusion is a divine act which impacts the self directly.

Hence the irritation caused to representatives of the Carmelite school by spiritual directors who, on the basis of their own experience or that of those they were guiding, thought 'acquired contemplation' possible. 'Acquired contemplation' would be when a certain stillness in prayer becomes habitual as people seek to simplify their meditative activity and by willed acts of prayer-filled attention to God—acts of adoration, contrition, thanksgiving, supplication—focus that activity as intensely as possible on God, in and for himself. This, however, is not yet contemplation as Teresa and John of the Cross would understand it. Speaking from a close acquaintance with their writings, Knowles finds it at best, and in some cases, a 'disposition' for contemplation. It is a sort of praying that makes someone readier to receive contemplation should the gift of contemplation, *per improbabile*, be infused. Knowles did not expect that many Christians would prove able to practise 'acquired contemplation' in such a way as to render them directly open to the infused gift of contemplative prayer. 'It is only when the prayer of recollection has become settled and pure, maintained through aridities and distractions for long, that it can be regarded as in any sense a disposition for infused contemplation.[14] ' Few people, he suspected, would find themselves in this situation. Few would stay the course.

Bouyer's view is very different. Writers who introduced the notion of acquired contemplation were not imprudently innovating. They were getting back to the more ancient notion of meditation and prayer found in the Fathers of the Church. In Bouyer's judgment, all prayer, when rightly conceived, opens the way for contemplation. And the same is true of all meditation so long as it is rightly conceived likewise. In a passage that angered Jesuit readers who saw in it an attack on the Ignatian *Exercises*, Bouyer defended the supporters of acquired contemplation not least for their more holistic view of the meditation that should be feeding prayer at large—including, then, via active prayer, contemplative prayer itself:

> It is these same writers, generally speaking, who have worked out a view of meditation which may not coincide in every respect with that of Antiquity, but which, nevertheless, no longer reduces meditation to [a] conjunction of deductive reasonings and artificially evoked phantasms, for the purpose of a kind of forcing of the will. In fact, as soon as we get away from these psychological gymnastics and try to bring meditation back to a simple and organic view of the great truths of the faith—or better still, of the mystery of Christ... it can be said that the effort proper to meditation, far from being opposed to the 'passivity' that marks

---

[14] Knowles, *What is Mysticism?*, p. 88.

contemplation, rather leads to it of its own accord and lends it a helping hand.[15]

The essential question is 'whether meditation is to be organized in function of essentially fragmentary views of Christian dogma and picturesque but grossly concretized imaginative representations of the Christian reality, or whether, rather, beneath all the dogmas, beneath all the realities of the Gospel, it should tend to embrace one single mystery—the unity of this mystery being neither that of an abstract concept nor of a picture highly individualized in terms of time and space, but the mysterious living unity of a divine incarnate Person and of the design for our salvation in which he reveals Himself to us in giving Himself to our faith and our love.'[16] In other words: the Word, the Trinitarian Son, inviting us to share divine life.

Bouyer warned against an unnuanced use of the terms 'passive' and 'active' as applied to prayer. Just as it would be wrong to regard meditation as purely the fruit of human autonomy, so likewise it would be a mistake to regard contemplation as so divine as not to require the collaboration of human powers. Thus on meditation it can safely be said that '[o]ur own activity only exists and proves fruitful in prayer to the exact measure of the activity of grace in us',[17] and on contemplation that 'if God acts in us, it is in no way somehow to substitute for us, but rather to foster an activity which, when it manifests itself, is not less our own from having come wholly from him'.[18]

---

[15] Bouyer, *Introduction to Spirituality*, pp. 73–4.
[16] Ibid., p. 74.
[17] Ibid., p. 76.
[18] Ibid., pp. 75–6.

Admittedly, Christian antiquity was not totally unaware of *all* distinction between active and passive in this context. It was not hostile to any idea whatsoever of varying 'depths' of prayerfulness, shall we say. A number of ancient ecclesiastical writers have their own take on this. Bouyer provided four examples, two from the East, two from the West.

For the East, for instance in the fifth-century *Macarian Homilies* — generally ascribed to an unknown Syrian author who took as his pseudonym one of the most celebrated Egyptian desert fathers of an earlier generation, Macarius the Great — there are two sorts of prayer. One kind is 'laborious', an 'ascetic effort', and 'pursued in relative darkness'.[19] The other sort is the fruit of the effort that has gone into the first kind of prayer. This second sort of prayer comes over from Macarius's descriptions as 'an ardent, luminous prayer in which the soul expands in a sense of abundance created in it by the Spirit'.[20] Macarius regarded such jubilant contemplative prayer as a taste of Heaven, a foretaste of the experience of the Age to Come.[21]

More important for later tradition, as a witness to differing kinds of prayer is that other anonymous Syrian writer, Dionysius the Areopagite, who in his treatise *The Mystical Theology* spoke in influential language of three great stages in prayer: purification, illumination, union. We purify ourselves so as to be the more receptive to the illumination which comes from meditation on Scripture, and such illumination, once it shapes our prayer, is ordered to final union with God himself, a

---

[19] Ibid., p. 77.
[20] Ibid.
[21] See Marcus Plested, *The Macarian Legacy. The Place of Macarius-Symeon in the Eastern Christian Tradition* (Oxford: Oxford University Press, 2004).

contemplation of God in a darkness that comes from the excess of divine light.

Two Western witnesses, to parallel the choice of Dionysius and the author of the *Macarian Homilies* for the East, are Augustine and Gregory the Great. Augustine pictures meditation as a movement which ascends through the corporeal to the incorporeal, indeed to the Uncreated, in transitory moments of contemplation gaining a fleeting glimpse of the divine beauty, before falling back to the corporeal level. Yet by this experience the mind's desire for the uncreated beauty has been rekindled, and so the soul pursues the upward movement once again and with greater effectiveness. The best known account in Augustine's writing comes in Book X of the *Confessions* where he describes an experience of rapture he shared at Ostia with his mother Monica shortly before her death.[22] Comparing it with other allusions in Augustine's corpus, his biographer Serge Lancel remarks, 'With the "ecstasy of Ostia" we shall again find the same gradual rise and the same return, with its accompanying powerful longing'.[23]

St Gregory the Great speaks in similar terms of a contemplative 'excess' whereby the soul is briefly ravished, taken away from itself, and indeed from all distinct thoughts of whatever is created. It soon returns to earth but does so altered inasmuch as it is reinvigorated in its effort to reach the vision of God in heaven. In his study of monastic culture in the West, *The Love of Learning and the Desire for God*, Dom Jean Leclerq summed up Gregory's teaching when he explained:

---

[22] Augustine, *Confessions*, X, 65.
[23] Serge Lancel, *Saint Augustine*. English trans. (London: SCM Press, 2002), p. 86.

> The soul... is [now] in a deeper, stronger state of humility, humility born of the knowledge of God ... The soul, illuminated by God's light, the soul which knows God, perceives in itself all that is impure and contrary to God. Thus it is confirmed in humility, in the same attitude which had been the point of departure and the fundamental reason for its initial flight towards God.[24]

In both of these Latin doctors, St Augustine and St Gregory, a glimpse given by God of himself complements human effort and restimulates it.

If we apply to these schemes the language of activity and passivity, the contemplative does not seem to become, under the impact of divine action, simply inert. Rather, she is acting more than ever—but she is also conscious that God is engaged in making possible in her the willing and the doing by which she acts. Looked at through the lens of dogmatic theology, contemplation can be regarded as the proper development of the original act of Christian faith in its adherence to the Word of God, since that act constitutes the beginning of glory. In the words of St Thomas, faith 'makes those realities we hope for, our future blessedness, exist in us inchoatively'.[25] The act of faith relates us ultimately to the vision of God, participation in which is the goal where revelation would lead us.[26] Contemplative prayer, or a set of contemplative moments in

---

[24] Jean Leclerq, OSB, *The Love of Learning and the Desire for God. A Study of Monastic Culture*. English trans. (New York: Fordham University Press, 1974, 2nd edition), p. 42.

[25] Thomas Aquinas, *Compendium theologiae*, I. 2; compare his *Summa theologiae*, Ia. IIae., q.1, a. 8, and *De veritate*, q. 14, a. 2.

[26] Jean-Pierre Torrell, OP, *Saint Thomas Aquinas*, vol. 2, *Spiritual Master*. English trans. (Washington, DC: Catholic University of America Press, 2003), pp. 14–15, 17–18.

prayer, is an anticipation, whether hugely powerful or relatively feeble, of that same vision. In this perspective, contemplation can be called the manifestation of the grace which is already hiddenly at work in meditation and prayer at large. It is that grace now showing itself for what it is. Until the life of glory this can hardly be a permanent condition. That does not undermine its importance. Contemplative experience stimulates a search for the face of God, the ultimate outcome of our assimilation of the mystery. Seeing the face of God is the final point of all ascetic striving and mystical aspiration. In the vision of God all creation will be given back to us again but in a new mode, as so many refractions of the divine glory.

✧ 4 ✧

Principles of Asceticism

WHAT IS NOW CALLED SPIRITUALITY or spiritual theology was once termed, from the seventeenth century onwards, 'ascetical and mystical theology'. As between the two parts, 'ascetical and mystical theology', *ascetical* theology is necessarily placed first, since, on the view of things implied by the phrase, asceticism is the indispensable preliminary to mysticism, which, therefore, has to be considered second. To understand asceticism, though, it is necessary not to lose sight of mysticism, its desired outcome. This must be borne in mind in any account of the 'principles of asceticism'.

The place of asceticism

Asceticism has a very large place in the spiritual literature of historic Christianity. 'The subject of combating the passions and training in the virtues', wrote Giorgios Mantzarides, 'occupies a central position in the teaching of the Fathers of the Church.' And Mantzarides went on, 'This is natural, because this is the area where man's disposition to co-operate with the grace of God for his salvation and renewal is manifest in the most decisive way'.[1] The earliest recorded use

---

[1] Mantzarides, *Orthodox Spiritual Life*, p. 113.

of the Latin word *spiritualitas* bears out his claim. It comes in a letter from a celebrated (not to say notorious) early-fifth-century ascetic master, Pelagius — forever associated in the West with the 'Pelagian heresy'. The letter was once ascribed to the Latin doctor St Jerome, a testimony to the high esteem in which later generations held it. The Benedictine historian of mediaeval spirituality Dom Jean Leclerq describes its author's choice of subject-matter in favourable terms. The topic of the letter is 'leading that life according to the Spirit to which [a Christian] has been initiated from his baptism and which implies fidelity to the divine law [in] the effort to practise detachment from sin and attachment to God'.[2] The subject, then, is detachment from sin and attachment to God, based on baptismal initiation and the keeping of the Law of Christ.

Pelagius's text, as explicated by Dom Leclerq, could serve quite well as a definition of the ascetic life, seen as the preamble to the mystical life, in the tradition of the Great Church in the East as well as in the West. On the ascetic way, we seek to become detached from sin, and attached to God, thanks to baptismal grace and our own efforts to keep the Law of Christ. And if this is so, asceticism has surely to count as a major part of spirituality, *spiritualitas*. That in turn indicates a need to identify the general 'principles' of such asceticism: asceticism understood as the practical way of becoming detached from sin and attached to God, through both divine grace and human effort.

---

[2] Jean Leclerq, OSB, 'Spiritualitas', in *Studi medievali*, 3rd series, 3 (1962), pp. 279–96, and here at p. 280. He points out that this is a relatively rare use in Latin patristics or the Latin Middle Ages, where, although *spiritualitas* sometimes denotes the struggle for perfection, it more commonly serves as a synonym for immateriality.

Principles of Asceticism

Where shall we find in Scripture a good introduction to the principles underlying such asceticism? Bouyer finds an opening in an oracle from the prophet Hosea. 'She [i.e. Israel] has not remembered that it was I who gave her her cheese, wine and oil, who gained her the silver and gold that have been devoted to Baal (Hosea 2:10).' In Bouyer's opinion, 'Here we find for the first time, along with the renewed affirmation that all these things are good since they come from God, the new affirmation that man, being what he is, becomes as it were stifled by the enjoyment of them. He forgets that God is behind His gifts. Instead of God, he confects those false gods who are only the personification of his appetites, of his slavery to his own riches.'[3] Only by deprivation for a while of these good things will man return to his senses, really recognizing the Giver. Hence Hosea's prophecy that Israel must return for a while to the desert. For his part, von Balthasar remarks: 'We must relinquish things that are ours because they take up space which God's Word claims in us. Furthermore, the Word is divisive: it is a "sword" and "fire", and it is with these distinctive characteristics that it must conquer territory within us, otherwise it cannot exist at all.'[4] These two twentieth-century spiritual writers have essentially the same advice. Something has to go if there is to be space for a jealous God. Something must be relinquished if there is to be room for God.

Scanning the Scriptures in this light furnishes plenty of examples. In the Old Testament, Isaiah, Jeremiah, the 'Suffering Servant' of the Book of Isaiah, Job, and the 'poor ones' (the *anawim*) of the Book of Psalms: all in their different ways either praise or exemplify

---

[3] Bouyer, *Introduction to Spirituality*, p. 129.
[4] von Balthasar, *Prayer*, p. 25.

those whose only consolation is their reliance on God alone. The apocalyptic theme in the Book of Daniel confirms this emerging picture by surrendering any idea of establishing ourselves at home in the present age of the world. In the New Testament, the Lord himself, at the Incarnation, appears among the *anawim*, the child of one who professed virginity, and after the Epiphany an infant in desperate straits—as he would remain throughout his life. Pre-announced by a desert-dwelling ascetic, his message includes the theme of self-renunciation or taking up a cross. It will fall to his born-out-of-time apostle St Paul, in the Letter to the Philippians, to interpret such renunciation as a life of *kenosis*, of self-emptying, in imitation of the Incarnation itself.

For the ancient Church, the life of the martyrs embodied such letting-go the good things of this world. Not settling down comfortably in the world—and thus asceticism—was a preparation for the martyrdom that might well be coming. Meanwhile asceticism itself could be, as origen suggested at the close of his *Exhortation to Martyrdom*, a sort of bloodless martyrdom,[5] what the Celtic tradition of the later patristic period will call 'white martyrdom'. It is the martyrdom of those from whom the red blood from veins and arteries has not been required.

On Bouyer's analysis, Christian asceticism entails a fundamental optimism about the world—for there really are many 'good things' in it, combined with a conditional pessimism about the world—how the use of the world's good things might affect us now. In addition to the couplet 'fundamental optimism and condi-

---

[5] Louis Bouyer, *The Spirituality of the New Testament and the Fathers*. English trans. (London: Burns and Oates, 1963), p. 210.

tional pessimism', Bouyer also uses the pairing 'metaphysical optimism and historical pessimism'. As he explains: 'A metaphysical optimism, since everything is good in itself, in our own nature and in the universe, our body as well as our soul, matter as well as spirit, for everything has been willed and created by God. A historical pessimism, inasmuch as sin has vitiated the very conditions of our spiritual life, our natural relationships with things.'[6] This is why a new start must be made, a death to the goods that screen God from us, but also a resurrection to those goods insofar as they are brought back into harmony with God in a changed life.

A suitable anthropology

This new condition of ascetically achieved harmony with God, even while we are living in this world, corresponds to the basic structure of Christian anthropology. The whole of man, not the body only, nor the soul or spirit only, must be rightly aligned with God's purpose. St Paul wrote to the church in Thessalonica, 'May the God of peace Himself sanctify you completely, and may He keep in wholeness your spirit, your soul and your body without reproach at the Parousia of our Lord Jesus Christ (I Thessalonians 5:23). Principles of asceticism are always closely bound up with anthropology.

For the Fathers of the Church and the later divines, Christian anthropology can either be presented as bipartite, body, *soma*, and soul, *psyche* (this is more common in the West), or alternatively it can be pre-

[6] Bouyer, *Introduction to Spirituality*, p. 143.

sented as tripartite, body, soul, and spirit, *pneuma* (this is more common in the East, and appears already, of course, in the citation from Paul given in the paragraph above). The explanation for the seeming discrepancy lies in the fact that *pneuma*, 'spirit', can be regarded either as transcending human nature—hence the bipartite account for which it suffices to speak of our nature as body-and-soul, or, alternatively, *pneuma* can be considered integral to human nature—hence the tripartite account where there is not only body and soul but spirit as well.[7]

To a degree, these two schemes—bipartite and tripartite—can be reconciled, as Bouyer is quick to point out. His way of doing so is not the only version, but it adds up. In biblical discourse 'spirit' means in the first place the Spirit of God, the Spirit communicated as a gift at Adam's creation. Without the divine Spirit man cannot be what he is meant to be. The more the human being integrates the Spirit into his life, the more the soul, in vivifying the body, becomes itself vivified by the Spirit. And the more the soul lives in that way, the more it takes on a condition of 'spiritual' life, an existence precisely as 'spirit'.[8] Here, then, the spirit is a new mode of existence the soul can make its own, and which, through the soul, the body can make its own likewise.

Unfortunately, anthropologies at variance with this biblical vision of human wholeness—anthropologies that, generally speaking, issue from *philosophical* sources—sometimes influenced the writers of the

---

[7] For a very full discussion, extending from Paul to the modern period see Henri de Lubac, 'Anthropologie trinitaire' in his *Théologie dans l'histoire, I. La lumière du Christ* (Paris: Desclée de Brouwer, 1990), pp. 115–200.

[8] Bouyer, *Introduction to Spirituality*, pp. 144–5.

patristic Church to their detriment. That could affect their understanding of the principles of asceticism. The youthful von Balthasar thought that patristic *ressourcement*, though undoubtedly essential, not in *every* respect a desirable programme for the Church and theology today.[9] But possibly he overlooked a point. The psychology of pagan writers may be right even when their anthropology is wrong. 'While Christian spirituality could not adopt the dualistic metaphysics implicit in Platonic or Neo-Platonic conceptions, it had no reason to reject the psychological observations on which this metaphysics was founded ... The fact that, according to the Bible, the body was made for the soul in no way prevents us from recognizing that, today, in the concrete condition of man as he is, the body is a drag on the soul. Consequently, although the soul deceives itself in believing that it will find God in simply rediscovering itself [this was the metaphysical mistake of the Platonist tradition], it is no less true that it will not find God and it will not rediscover itself without a certain liberation from the chains by which the body, and the world along with that body, hold it down [this was the correct psychological intuition of Platonism] — even though it is also quite true that these chains have been forged by the soul itself.'[10] In the biblical picture, the soul that has withdrawn from subjection to the divine Spirit cannot bring the body to its own level. Such a soul subverts the body's own integrity, and, in so doing, succumbs to instinctual impulses in anarchic array. So an ascetical programme,

---

[9] Hans Urs von Balthasar, 'The Fathers, the Scholastics, and Ourselves', *Communio* 24 (1997), pp. 377–96. The German original dates from 1939.
[10] Bouyer, *Introduction to Spirituality*, p. 149.

a programme of grace-assisted effort, is altogether necessary if body, soul and spirit are to be brought into harmonious unity, rather than a coalition of chaos.

Asceticism in West and East

For the sake of such a programme Christian West and Christian East have set out the principles involved. Western asceticism is dominated by Augustine's writing, while the East owes almost equally much to the fourth-century Greek-speaking monk Evagrius of Pontus.

Augustine is too well known to need an introduction even had he not already been mentioned in my text. But a caveat from David Knowles will be in order. In Knowles's view, Augustine really 'had no occasion to give elaborate instructions on prayer and on the degrees of the spiritual life'.[11] Rather, he did something else. First, he described a number of his own spiritual experiences, some of which occurred either before, or shortly after, his conversion and baptism—when a mature grasp of asceticism as a precondition to the life of union with God could hardly be expected of him.[12] Secondly, he laid out a programme for Christian formation which, in Knowles's words, 'in its higher reaches merged into a psychological and

---

[11] David Knowles, *The English Mystical Tradition* (London: Burns and Oates, 1964 [1961]), p. 25. Knowles has in view the contrary thesis as stated in Cuthbert Butler, OSB, *Western Mysticism. The Teaching of SS. Augustine, Gregory and Bernard on Contemplation and the Contemplative Life* (London: Constable, 1927, 2nd edition]).

[12] Knowles, *The English Mystical Tradition*, p. 26.

spiritual ascent towards God'.[13] Augustine recommended the reflective person to move from the image of the Trinity in the self—in one's own interior powers of remembering, knowing and willing or loving—to the uncreated Model or Archetype of these powers that is the Trinity in its own blessed being. Here too, according to Knowles, Augustine was to a considerable extent 'describing the psychological findings of his own life'.[14] Thirdly and finally, Augustine offered an account of the relation between the active life and the contemplative life as 'states of life', ways of discipleship, in the Church. These elements from Augustine's writings were subsequently recycled by mediaeval Western writers—the Franciscan St Bonaventure and the group known as 'the Victorines', theologically minded Augustinian canons of the Abbey of St Victor outside Paris come to mind. Bonaventure and the Victorines re-deployed Augustine's material in the service of a systematic view of the contemplative life understood precisely as a life that is ordered to mystical prayer. But for Augustine himself—as is made plain by his discussion of the active and contemplative lives embodied in the apostles Peter and John or the Bethany sisters Martha and Mary—the contemplative life is not *as such* a mystical life. As Augustine sees it, the contemplative life is essentially a 'life of study, meditation and reflection', the 'Platonic and Aristotelian life of contemplation translated into Christian terms. It is not the life of a mystic as such but the life of one given to the consideration of Scripture and theology as understood in Augustine's scheme of the Christian's intellectual ascent to God; its goal is indeed the

---

[13] Ibid.
[14] Ibid., p. 27.

vision of God, dimly here and clearly hereafter, but it is a way of life in its external totality, the life of a whole class of Christians, not the mystical progress of divinely called individuals. While it might foster a life of mystical prayer, this would not be its direct or inevitable end.'[15] Knowles is telling us that, owing to the specialized foci of Augustine's interests when touching on questions of the ascetical and mystical way—foci which are, respectively, autobiographical, educational, and ecclesiological—we should not look to Augustine for general guidance in the relation of asceticism and mysticism.

As to the Oriental writers, Evagrius, as already mentioned, is the historic starting-point for their articulation of ascetic principles. The other Desert Fathers left behind sayings or anecdotes of their actions, not theoretical statements of principle. There is no doubt about Evagrius's intention, as there *is* a doubt (if Knowles is right) about Augustine's. Evagrius was consciously laying out a scheme for the development of an ascetical and mystical life.

In Evagrius's anthropological scheme, the soul, *psyche*, comes midway between the body, *soma*, and the spiritual mind, *nous*, where the image of God is located and which Evagrius takes to be the proper 'place' (as he puts it) of the presence of God. I translated *nous* there by 'spiritual mind', and in fact the term *nous* plays much the same role in Evagrius's anthropology as 'spirit' does in other Christian authors of the same period. The *nous* is where God's Holy Spirit can make himself present, just as the *pneuma*—a new mode of existence for the soul—serves that function in other writers. The word *nous* in patristic Greek has quite

---

[15] *Ibid.*, p. 28.

different overtones from our terms 'mind' or 'intellect' and their derivatives 'mental' and 'intellectual'. '*Noesis*, the typical activity of *nous*, is a kind of thought that is much deeper, much simpler, much more contemplative, much more participatory, than what we in the twenty-first century, as post-Cartesian humans, normally consider thinking to be.'[16] In a religious context, that makes it easy for the word *nous* to take on connotations of openness to God and his Spirit, just like *pneuma* elsewhere.

On the Evagrian scheme: if, as a result of passions issuing from the body and registered by the soul, the soul comes to ignore God and think only of the body, then the divine Antagonist, Satan, holds it in servitude, disabling its experiential knowledge of God. At all costs the soul must free itself from the passions. The struggle to do so is what Evagrius calls the 'active life' (clearly, this bears not at all on Augustine's use of that term). The aim is the achievement of *apatheia*—liberation from bondage to passions—whereupon *psyche* can tend wholly towards *nous* and therefore to the divine presence. Here the 'active life' is in fact asceticism.

Before there is any question of contemplating God 'noetically', through contemplative participation, the soul, once emancipated from the passions, must learn to look aright at God's world, at God's creation. Origen, not a monastic but respected by Evagrius for his spiritual doctrine, had written on this topic in his *Commentary on the Song of Songs*. 'Since ... it is impossible for a man living in the flesh to know anything of matters hidden and invisible unless he has apprehended some image and likeness thereto among things visible, I think that He who made all things in wisdom

---

[16] Louth, *The Origins of the Christian Mystical Tradition*, p. xvi.

so created all the species of visible things upon earth that He placed in them some teaching and knowledge of things invisible and heavenly whereby the human mind might mount to spiritual understanding and seek the grounds of things in heaven.'[17] According to Origen, the Word of God has left signs of himself in the world around us: little (or not so little) created 'words', that are immanent in things, inhere in them as the ground of their intelligibility. These words stem from the great Uncreated Word. From the all-creating Logos with a capital 'L' come these little *logoi* with a lower-case 'l', these created words. In his treatise on prayer von Balthasar would speak in Romantic, not Platonist, idiom of 'the words strewn throughout creation, stammered and whispered; the words of nature, in macrocosm and microcosm; the words uttered by the flowers and animals; words of overpowering beauty and of debilitating terror'.[18] To discern these *logoi* implanted in things by the Logos—to see ordinary things aright—becomes, in the Evagrian programme, a normal part of ascetical training. Natural contemplation, a disinterested perception of things as creatively envisaged by God, is evidence of serious movement towards the passionless state. To be able to look steadily at, say, a bluebell or a kestrel, not distracted by anything, not even the associations of the flower or the bird, but to see it for itself as an expression of the creative divine Mind, this already requires ascetic training and constitutes a form of natural contemplation. The nineteenth-century English Jesuit Gerard Manley Hopkins gives us examples of

---

[17] Origen, *Commentary on the Song of Songs* III. 12.
[18] von Balthasar, *Prayer*, p. 19.

how he sought to do this in his poetry (bird),[19] and prose (flower).[20]

The role of the heart

But the *apatheia* or passionlessness which corrects distorted emotions in the body and unhelpful images or impressions in the soul is desirable for more than simply taking an unimpeded look at the world around us. Such *apatheia* is a necessity if someone is to be fitted to enjoy the knowledge of God, and truly to make their own the charity of God: the love 'poured into our hearts', according to St Paul, 'by the Holy Spirit' (Romans 5:5).

'Into our hearts': these words from the Letter to the Romans are a cue for Bouyer to bring in the first of his *correctores* for the Evagrian doctrine.[21] In the *Macarian Homilies*—enormously influential as these were in the Byzantine East—Evagrius's key term *nous* is replaced by *kardia*, the 'heart'. Macarius understands the 'heart' neither as the highest condition of our faculties (which *nous* or *pneuma* could be), nor as sheer affective feeling (which is what modern idiom would suggest). Rather, in the *Homilies*, the heart is the locus of the powers of the human person as a whole. There is a cross-cultural link here to Augustine for whom *cor*, the Latin for 'heart', functions in this same 'Macarian' way. Augus-

---

[19] *The Poems of Gerard Manley Hopkins*, ed. W. H. Gardner and N. H. Mackenzie (London: Oxford University Press, 1967, 4th edition), p. 69.
[20] *The Journals and Papers of Gerald Manley Hopkins*, ed. Humphrey House and Graham Storey (London: Oxford University Press, 1966), entry for 18 May 1870.
[21] Bouyer, *Introduction to Spirituality*, p. 151.

tine's *Confessions* opens with an address to God which includes the famous words: 'Our heart is restless until it begins to find rest in you'.[22] Serge Lancel commented: '*Our* heart is restless, says Augustine, bearing witness on behalf of all mankind in fraternal humility and using to express the seat of this existential unrest the word "heart" which, taken from the Psalms, so often bursts into his text to designate the moral centre of the human being, simultaneously body and soul'.[23]

In the *Macarian Homilies*, asceticism means learning how to invite Jesus into the heart, so understood, there to be the master of all the ascetic's powers, whether spiritual, psychological or physical. This notion of the entry of Jesus into the heart, the true centre of the personality, will provide the strongly Christocentric element in the later tradition of Greek asceticism, and is something I shall return to later.

Enstasis and *ekstasis*

Bouyer's other 'corrector' of Evagrius is Dionysius the Areopagite.[24] The movement of the soul towards God, described as a journey through the stages of purgation, illumination and union, must be not just 'enstatic', moving inwards—whether this be conceived with Evagrius as into the *nous* or, for that matter, with Macarius as into the *kardia*. That journey must also be 'ecstatic', moving outwards, moving beyond everything created, itself included, if it is to find God.

[22] Augustine, *Confessions* I. 1.
[23] Lancel, *Saint Augustine*, p. 209.
[24] Bouyer, *Introduction to Spirituality*, pp. 151–2.

This has little to do with ecstasy in the sense of rapture, being caught up into a glimpse of what is normally reserved for heaven, as with Augustine and Gregory the Great in the West. Instead, it is a permanent attitude of 'standing outside', *ek-stasis*, moving out beyond the self and ultimately out beyond all finite expressions of God in the world.

The passions

At the beginning of this chapter, I quoted Mantzarides' description of the ascetical life as combat with the passions in service of growth in the virtues. In discussion of ascetic principles, 'passions' (in Greek *pathē*) are best thought of not as 'emotions', in the contemporary use of that word—too 'broad brush', and too neutral—to serve. In the Eastern Christian tradition, unless qualification be added, 'passions' are pejorative. In Staniloae's elucidation, they are 'the movements of sinful appetites' together with 'ideas' or 'impressions' that 'appear in the mind', eliciting the passions, accompanying them, and, perhaps, being retained in their wake.[25] Such 'impressions' can stay with us as unhelpful presences even when the appetites have been quieted or corrected.

The passions in question—signs of a sensibility gone awry—are unthinkable without the Fall. For Staniloae, as for his principal patristic source, Maximus—who synthesized Evagrius, Macarius and Dionysius—they must be distinguished from 'natural', God-given, passions (here the meaning of the noun is governed by the qualifying adjectives) which befit our bodily nature,

[25] Staniloae, *Orthodox Spirituality*, p. 25.

and assist its preservation. The innocence of animals in their instinctual life is replicated in *homo sapiens* so long as these natural passions remain within bounds that serve biological existence. But the disorder of the Fall changed this, distorting the natural passions and introducing entirely non-natural passions as well.

Firstly, then, on this analysis, the natural passions can be distorted. As Staniloae explains: 'Because man is spirit too and so has an irreducible aspiration for the infinite, he can associate this aspiration of his with the natural, biological passions, transforming them into unnatural passions, in other words exaggerated passions, pierced by an infinite thirst for satisfaction.'[26] When Adam falls the natural passions are not unaffected. They themselves undergo a fall of a kind acquiring as they do a kind of false infinitude. Sex, or food and drink, were never meant to be our gods.

There is worse to come. The fall of the natural passions generates an egotism which goes on to produce unconditionally unnatural passions: passions, namely, that have no pre-lapsarian, no divinely created, counterpart. Examples are such emotional-intellectual complexes as vanity and pride. These passions are unconditionally non-natural since unconnected with our biology—unlike, for example, gluttony and lust which at least have a physiological excuse.[27]

---

[26] *Ibid.*, pp. 84–5.
[27] Since in the Byzantine spiritual tradition these are counted as passions rather than vices, Staniloae could not treat the passions as 'psycho-physiological data, which in themselves are neither good nor bad'; Torrell, *Saint Thomas Aquinas*, vol. 2, *Spiritual Master*, p. 261. St Thomas, by contrast, wishes, as he says explicitly, to 'give the name of passion simply to all the movements of the sensitive appetite', *Summa theologiae*, Ia. IIae., q. 24, a. 3.

Whether by damaging the natural passions or by arising independently, under the pressure of egoism, as post-lapsarian innovations, the fallen passions have certain effects in common. They overthrow the internal hierarchy which is a given of our nature as creatures composed of body, soul, and spirit. They dislocate the harmony among these powers and do so in a way beyond the ability of natural therapy to heal. They thus constitute a form of slavery.

It remains the case, however, that emotion or sensibility can not only contribute to the spiritual life but even constitute the 'basis' of its 'growth'.[28] That is because the passions can be altered—indeed transfigured, spiritualized—by a transfer of their energy to relation with God. Rather as in the Freudian theory of the sublimation of libido, asceticism serves the process of our purification by using the passions to turn the self in a Godward direction. 'It is the whole man who must be Christianized; the human being goes towards God with all that is in him.'[29]

The enemy is not so much, then, passions in themselves as what the Byzantine tradition calls *prospatheia*, enslavement to the passions in which—in Staniloae's words—we spend our lives 'waiting for and seeking pleasure and in the fear of present and future pain'.[30] To become available to God it is necessary to be free of the care, the anxiety, that the impassioned or 'prospathetic' state entails.

Staniloae will devote some one hundred and twenty pages to the discussion of the nature of purification from the passions, and his account corresponds to the

---

[28] Staniloae, *Orthodox Spirituality*, p. 86.
[29] Torrell, *Saint Thomas Aquinas*, vol. 2, *Spiritual Master*, p. 262.
[30] Staniloae, *Orthodox Spirituality*, p. 115.

first of Dionysius's three stages of growth towards God, the purgative way. After an initial treatment of the passions, natural and unnatural, their causes and effects, he considers in turn faith as the ultimate basis of their purification, and then such helps in the overcoming of the unnatural passions as the fear of God and the thought of judgment, repentance, self-control, the guarding of the mind or the thoughts, longsuffering,

hope, meekness, and humility. Finally, he comes to 'dispassion' or freedom from passion which is itself the desired outcome of the attitudes, practices and virtues he has just discussed.

In Chapter 6 of this book we shall consider more in detail how the way of purification unfolds. In Chapter 5, however, I want to look, with Bouyer's help, at the differentiation of asceticism brought about by the existence of different groups of believers in the Church.

✧ 5 ✧

Asceticism: Monastic, Lay and 'Pastoral'

THIS CHAPTER considers three groups in the Church and how the principles of asceticism might apply to them. The groups are: monastics, layfolk, and those engaged in an active—Bouyer calls it a 'pastoral'—'apostolate' as ordained men or religious sisters and brothers. I shall be especially dependent in this chapter on Bouyer's account which is as thoughtful as it is robust.

Monastic asceticism

The most fundamental type of Christian calling is the monastic vocation. A monk or nun has a vocation to consecrated virginity combined with poverty of goods in obedience to some sort of rule for Gospel living—though this would not be, at the beginnings of the Church, a 'rule' in a literary sense as with the Rule of St Augustine or the Rule of St Benedict.

The monastic calling is the most fundamental of all vocations because it is the simplest of all Christian lives. It is a form of discipleship not yet complicated (if also enriched) by such additions as marriage, the ownership of property—especially productive property, admission to Holy Orders, or the taking on of some specific apostolate in the Church.[1] Since it is the most basic Christian life-form, we shall not be surprised to find that monasticism provides the most basic form of Christian asceticism as well.

Monastic poverty, chastity and obedience furnish the structure for a life of continence—or what is called in patristic Greek *enkrateia*. Continence, taken in the wide ascetic sense, extends far beyond the sexual domain. It denotes, in Bouyer's words, 'resistance to the exaggerated desires of fallen human nature', with a view to regaining 'the dominion of the spirit within us (the Spirit of God taking possession of our spirit)'.[2] This will mean, then, a dominion of the spirit over the passions, those disordered sensuous appetites and the memory-traces they leave behind as future instruments for 'perverse spiritual suggestions' of whatever kind.[3] Continence in its widest sense—the *enkrateia* sense—is meant to produce *apatheia*, literally 'passionlessness', the word Evagrius had chosen: meaning, of course, not insensibility but, rather—in Bouyer's helpful definition—the 'mastery of our sensibility by charity, *agape*, in a soul given up in complete obedience to the demands of faith'.[4] *Apatheia* in the Evagrian sense well sums up the demands of the ascetic life seen as detachment from sin and attachment to God.

It is in this perspective that Bouyer discusses the ascetical value of poverty, chastity, and obedience as practised in the monastic life, the most foundational, if

[1] See Aidan Nichols, OP, *What is the Religious Life? From the Gospels to Aquinas* (Leominster: Gracewing, 2015), where I make this case.
[2] Bouyer, *Introduction to Spirituality*, p. 198.
[3] Ibid., p. 203.
[4] Ibid.

rudimentary, version of Christian discipleship.[5] Poverty, which Bouyer connects to the monastic practice of fasting, returns the monk to simple living, where even basic satisfactions are held in check by periodic abstinence from food. Chastity, which he links especially with the monastic practice of vigil—prolonged meditation on the Word of God—aims to disengage the will from absorption in pleasure. The sort of chastity that is expressed in habitual vigil makes the monk wakefully alert—rather than immersed by the spirit of the world in soporific forgetfulness of God. Obedience, which Bouyer ties to the monastic practice of docile attention to a spiritual father, enables the monk to 'distinguish the attractions which really come from the divine Spirit from the subtle temptations of the demon, or simply from the hypocritical assertions of his own will', and thus tends to restore 'true freedom, the freedom of those immediately led by the Spirit of God'.[6]

There is, plainly, a degree of artificiality in the way Bouyer links poverty, chastity and obedience to (respectively) fasting, vigil, and listening to a spiritual father. But the connexions he draws enable him to make a further point. The way of life specified by poverty, chastity and obedience is the concrete monastic way pioneered by the first Christian monks whose practices were aimed at change of life. His presentation of the asceticism involved in chastity, poverty and obedience terminates in a discussion of three wider themes, which are not so much practices as modes of advancing along the ascetic way. They are: first, holy warfare; secondly, interior peace or in the Greek

---

[5] Ibid., pp. 198–200.
[6] Ibid., p. 200.

term favoured by the Byzantine tradition *hēsykhia*; and thirdly, solitude or entry into the desert.

Holy warfare means fighting with the passions, yes, but it also means fighting with angelic powers. Here what the Desert Fathers have to say is readily compatible with the reports modern exorcists give about their own experiences. In the words of St Paul, 'we wrestle not against flesh and blood, but against principalities, against powers, against the rulers of the darkness of this world' (Ephesians 6:12). The fallen angels, which are spiritual intelligences, make use of our disordered thoughts so as to enslave the *nous*, the contemplatively thinking mind, and prevent it from being what it is meant to be, the locus or 'place' of the divine presence. In holy warfare spiritual combat can make use of physical austerities but essentially it is a struggle of faith. So its main weapons are prayer, meditation on the divine Word, and reliance on Jesus Christ who is in us through our sacramental participation in his Paschal mystery by Baptism, Chrismation and the Eucharist. Holy warfare seeks to deal with the usually unperceived slavery in which in many ways we are still held. In doing so, it looks to our often equally unperceived Deliverer: the Jesus who is present in the heart, at the centre of the self, which is how the *Macarian Homilies* envisage him. In the baptized he is enthroned as King.

After holy warfare, Bouyer's second mode of ascetic advance is *hēsykhia*, interior peace. He points out, reasonably enough, that war is always waged with a view to some sort of peace. The quieting of the soul which results from ascetic effort in holy warfare is not likely, though, to be the totality of the peace Christ came to bring. That the demons have, at least for the moment, retired confounded is a negative result. It is not the total positivity of the peace that passes all understanding. Further purification will be needed before the soul enters into the Sabbath repose described by Scripture — for instance in the Letter to the Hebrews (at 4:9–10). This God-filled peace will be the authentic contemplative *hēsykhia* described by the Byzantine spiritual writers. It will anticipate in this world the perfect peace of the Age to Come. That can only be relevant to the last chapter of this book, the topic of which is the *via unitiva*, the way of union.

The third major theme of ascetic advance is entry into solitude, going into the desert.[7] In the early Christian centuries, the pursuit of spiritual combat led early monks such as Anthony of Egypt into the literal desert, often dwelling at least for a time at the entrances to abandoned tombs. Death, with its seemingly permanent disintegration of body and soul, is where the reign of Satan is at its most palpable. So that is where pioneering Christian ascetics took their stand. But the desert is a larger space than pagan cemeteries. It is in solitude, when, in the absence of others, we imagine ourselves to be entirely our own masters, that we discover we are not so and can be surprised at the aggressiveness with which former sinful ways seek to return. So entry into the desert, whether the wilderness be literal or metaphorical, reactivates the holy warfare where gains in peaceful ('hesychastic') self-possession have earlier been made, and does so in a deeper and more demanding way. The monk who has entered the desert is peculiarly exposed. The danger of this situation explains the reserve of many monastic founders about immediate entry into the eremitical

---

[7] See Peter F. Anson, *The Call of the Desert* (London: SPCK, 1973, 2nd edition).

life, bypassing some period of time in a common life of ascetics together. But in the last analysis, whatever prudence may say, solitude will have to be confronted. In the great trial of dying, unavoidable for each of us at the end of our lives, we shall, in an important sense, be quite alone. But this too is an opportunity to find the Lord. 'The way of the desert is not so much flight from society and community, as finding a way to an oasis where one can be aware again of the ultimate reality of God.'[8]

There is nothing here about the monastic presbyter (the monk-priest) but one can easily understand the emergence of this figure in both West and East. The Jesuit patrologist Brian Daley explains: 'As a man of God whose life was dedicated to God's praise in a kind of continual sacrifice, [the monk-priest] seemed more suited than the ordinary parish pastor to offer Christ's Eucharistic sacrifice to the Father'.[9] The offering of the Holy Sacrifice could well be regarded as the 'culmination of a life of contemplative prayer', with Ordination 'a kind of sacramental seal placed on a holy life, for the benefit of the monastic community and for the deeper sanctification of the monk himself.'[10] The asceticism of the monastic presbyter remains simply that of monastics at large.

---

[8] Andrew Louth, *The Wilderness of God* (London: Darton, Longman and Todd, 2003, 2nd edition), p. 14.
[9] Brian E. Daly, 'The Ministry of Disciples: Historical Reflections on the Role of Religious Priests', *Theological Studies* 48 (1987), pp. 606–29, and here at p. 617.
[10] *Ibid.*, p. 618.

Lay asceticism

Of course not all members of the Church can live like monastics, even in periods when the *Catholica* is flourishing more vigorously than in the modern setting. So I move on to consider, in Bouyer's wake, what asceticism might be for the laity and for the 'active' life of clergy and religious. I begin with lay asceticism.

As already asserted, if the monastic life is the most basic form of Christian discipleship, the lay life typically complicates or enriches that life with, for example, marriage and parenthood or professional work. These of course have their own challenges, but this does not mean that deliberately adopted asceticism should not figure in lay existence. Ascetic practices like prayer, keeping vigil, and fasting, as well as continence in the more restricted sexual sense of that word are all still pertinent, as are the themes of ascetic advance in holy warfare, *hēsykhia*, and solitude. Of course taken by themselves these practices and themes cannot constitute the entirety of a lay spirituality. A lay spirituality needs to take into account the subject matter of Chapter 2, the liturgical—and therefore sacramental—context of the spiritual life. The spirituality of a married Christian will have to include all the dimensions the sacrament of Matrimony opens up in terms of the relations of the spouses, the nurture of a family, and the giving of neighbourly hospitality. Likewise, the spirituality of a celibate Christian who is not a monastic or a 'pastor' (or, for that matter, ordained at all) will have to include all the dimensions the sacrament of Confirmation—Chrismation—opens up in terms of the multitude of charisms that can come into play, involving as these do callings for different people to a variety of ways of embodying Kingdom-purposes in the world.[11]

But what we are thinking about now is, specifically, the *asceticism* of the laity, considered as a constituent feature of advance towards the mystical life. If the monastic life is the most basic version of Christian discipleship (which theologically it is), and if Christian asceticism has developed within this most basic version (which historically it has), then lay asceticism like the asceticism of the pastorally engaged priest or religious will consist in—so to speak—a selection from the monastic programme, suitably adapted. Yves Congar, a protagonist of the proper priestly, royal and prophetic place of the laity in the Church wrote, 'We agree with those who, giving the word its full theological exactness and implications, reject the idea of ... a "lay spirituality" (and likewise of 'a "spirituality" of the diocesan clergy' which are the words I replaced by dots in this citation).[12] Congar added that he also had 'every sympathy' for those who sought to identify elements of the common spirituality 'among parish priests, in the apostolate, among the laity'.[13]

> The monk or nun is simply a Christian who concentrates to the uttermost on the one thing necessary, without the primacy of which there is no Christian life worth the name; and in the same way the spiritual life of the priest is simply the intensification of Christian life ... But lay people

---

[11] A major theme in Pope John Paul II's 1988 Apostolic Exhortation *Christifideles laici*.

[12] Yves M.-J. Congar, OP, *Lay People in the Church. A Study for a Theology of the Laity*. English trans. (London: Bloomsbury, 1957), p. 379.

[13] Ibid.

do not take monastic vows and have neither the helps nor the obligations of monastic life; they do not celebrate the sacraments or exercise the spiritual fatherhood of the priestly order, with its difficult and rewarding demands ... Obviously their 'being in Christ', while of the same essence as the being in Christ of priests and monks, is not in its conditions and actual living exactly that of priests and monks.[14]

And this is why, so far as asceticism is concerned, selectivity and adaptation come into play.

Such selectivity, and adaptation, are well known in the tradition. Specific times of prayer in one's room, where in the words of the Lord in the Gospels, the Father sees in secret, have been recommended to the laity since at least the time of Tertullian in the third century.[15] Such times of private prayer might even be regarded as *more* important for those living in the world than they are for monastics whose whole life is organized in function of prayer. They can be thought of as brief yet regular experiences of vigil. Tertullian had more especially in mind taking some minutes every night off the hours of sleep;[16] those with babies to look after might find this especially easy to achieve.

As to fasting, Christ connects it with prayer when prescribing for all his disciples without exception. To remain hungry from time to time is a way of learning to give more attention to God, by reminding ourselves that our principal 'hunger' must be for God. A twentieth-century French grace before meals says, God, give

---

[14] *Ibid.*, pp. 379–80.
[15] Tertullian, *On Prayer*, 25.
[16] Bouyer, *Introduction to Spirituality*, p. 178.

food to the hungry, and give hunger for you to those who have food.

For non-monastics fasting will often be connected with almsgiving, as in the Lenten sermons of St Leo the Great, read extensively in the Roman Breviary at that time of year. Alms should be generous enough to make us suffer some want ourselves, which is how the poor can help us towards Heaven. Christian almsgiving should be *sacrificial* charity and this it cannot be unless it includes some real privation, some significant loss of income through substantial giving to others.

In itself, fasting is one form of continence in the wider sense of that word, the curtailing of unruly or excessive desires, where 'un-rule' or 'excess' is whatever blunts spiritual acuity. 'The person who is accustomed to give in immediately to any desire, even one which is in principle legitimate, will one day, almost inevitably, come to give in also to illegitimate desire.'[17] In saying so, Bouyer does not exclude abstinence from conjugal relations, and thus a practice of continence in the narrower, sexual, sense. Sexual expression, just because it is, of all activities, the most psychologically 'absorbing',[18] singles itself out for attention when what is sought is a life more focused on God. Erotic 'fasting' helps the married to enter a solitude that can deepen prayer, and spiritualize their union. It has been a recommended practice to abstain from conjugal relations in the penitential seasons or on the vigils of the great feasts which, historically, are also times of fasting from food.

With all these forms of lay asceticism, 'discretion' is the key term used by the ascetic writers—meaning by that a suitable discernment of how best to apply

[17] Ibid., p. 182.
[18] Ibid.

asceticism to one's own life. Asceticism is not an end in itself. It is a means of subverting the hegemony of passions symptomatic of egoism, for the sake of the charity that will result. That is the message of the tradition, from Evagrius to Maximus the Confessor and the twentieth-century exponents of traditional asceticism's rationale.

Pastoral asceticism

There remains to be discussed the question of the asceticism of the non-monastic clergy, and of lay religious engaged in the 'active' or 'apostolic' life. Bouyer's name for this is 'pastoral asceticism', chiefly because it takes place out and about in the Church and the world. He regards such asceticism as partaking of features of both the monastic and the lay asceticism already discussed.

In one sense, that makes his account admirably suited to the needs of the married clergy in the Eastern Catholic churches, and, for that matter, to former Anglican clergy with wives and families — as in the 'ordinariates' created by Pope Benedict XVI as well as the mainstream Latin Catholic dioceses. Bouyer was both knowledgeable about the Anglican tradition and sympathetic to much of its liturgical, theological and devotional characteristics, while his ecumenical credentials in relation to the Eastern Orthodox, the mother churches of Oriental Catholics, were altogether impeccable. But in the matter of priesthood, as will now be seen, his understanding of asceticism took him to a very different place.

It might be an idea, he thinks, if the only members of the Church to be ordained priest were monks proven by competent judges to have made substantial progress in the ascetic life. 'To confer the priesthood on a monk who has attained the full development of his ascetic life can in many respects be considered as the ideal.'[19] And he seeks to justify this claim.

> The essentially pastoral role of the priest, for the sake of which he has been entrusted with the power to teach and the power to consecrate, imposes on him, above all, a very special duty personally to assimilate the holy realities of which he is not only the guardian but the transmitter. Charged with proclaiming the Word, more than anyone else he must have begun by examining it, penetrating it, making it his own. Charged with dispensing the mysteries of Christ, he must have begun by being the first to live them.[20]

Such a one will teach the Word he has fully appropriated. He will celebrate the sacraments he has deeply prayed.

But would he be too different from his people? The question inevitably arises in the context of the pastoral—and, above all, the parochial—clergy. The parochial clergy are by definition pastorally engaged, for they exercise, under the supervision of a bishop, the 'shepherding' or 'royal' office of the ministerial priesthood. But though Bouyer's emphasis on the 'sanctifying' and 'teaching' roles of the presbyter reflects the Mendicant theology of the Middle Ages to which the 'governing' office was a matter of delegation by bishops, his 'pastoral' priest is nevertheless rubbing shoulders with the people, and would do so even more if in receipt of an official 'cure of souls'. Bouyer's thought-experiment would have been less striking had he asked whether only those living the 'mixed' con-

[19] *Ibid.*, p. 217.
[20] *Ibid.*

templative-active life should be ordained. But he goes the full mile. He asks whether the ordained should ideally be restricted to pure contemplatives selected for the high repute they enjoy in their own monasteries. In such monk-priests, manfully taking up pastoral tasks hitherto strange to them, spiritual graces could no doubt inculcate a profound sympathy with Christians living in the world. Yet precisely because these are hoped-for gifts of grace, and gifts, by definition, are not always forthcoming, the institutionalization of the ideal would probably be as imprudent as most certainly it is regrettable. So the danger of rendering the pastoral clergy too unworldly bids Bouyer pull on the rope and bring the kite he has flown down to the ground. It is why the need for a specifically 'pastoral' asceticism can be inferred.

However, Bouyer will not define such pastoral asceticism *over against* monastic asceticism. Once it is agreed that, theologically, monastic life is the most basic form of Christian discipleship, and that, historically, asceticism has been developed as a set of practices and themes proper to the monastic life, then it would be contradictory to treat the asceticism of any other group in the Church as actually opposed to the asceticism of monastics. Pastoral asceticism may well be different from monastic asceticism just as, so we have seen, lay asceticism differs from it in the way it selects and applies. But difference is not contrariety.

Indeed, Bouyer begins his account by remarking that, since transmission of the divine mysteries implies an especially effective reception of them, the pastoral ascetic should begin 'by placing himself, at least for a time, outside of the world and its ways'.[21] As in the

[21] *Ibid.*, p. 221.

Lenten preparation of catechumens for the sacraments of initiation, so should be the experience of an ordinand in a seminary or its equivalent. And as with the annual Lent each Christian takes on himself, so there should be a yearly return to retreat for non-monastics in Holy Orders—or for anyone else living an apostolic life in the explicit service of the Church.

Clerical celibacy is of course pertinent here. It is typical of the New Testament vis-à-vis the Old to exhibit 'the transfer of the centre of gravity of the ascetic life from poverty to continence, and particularly to voluntary virginity'.[22] With regard to Old Testament ascetics, the Nazarites, Elijah, John the Baptist we hear of a desert life-style but not of virginity as such. It is different in the teaching of the Messiah. The messianic age is one where all the most intimate human powers are refocused on the divine Bridegroom who is at the door in his human form, waiting to enter the house of the soul. But, even so, for the Christian pastor, as distinct from the monastic, a qualification must be entered.

> The monk, in becoming a monk, can have no other immediate objective other than his complete liberation from all earthly ties to be wholly Christ's. The priest, in accepting the priesthood and more particularly the charge of souls, equally consecrates himself wholly to Christ, but, directly and by that very fact, to Christ in his brothers and especially in those to whom he is sent. His celibacy, with all that it implies and that extends it, should therefore be not only a celibacy in view of intimacy with God, but a celibacy in view of

---

[22] *Ibid.*, p. 223.

being, as the apostle says, 'all things to all men for Christ'.[23]

In the life of a monk, the rationale for celibacy is exclusively a matter of Christological mysticism, in the life of a pastoral priest the rationale for celibacy is also availability to the people of God.

These are two inter-connected modes of charity (towards God, towards neighbour). They will inform together the journey that takes a priest on the purgative, illuminative and unitive ways. For Garrigou-Lagrange, so as to 'enlighten others', a presbyter should be on the illuminative way, a bishop on the unitive way throughout their ministries.[24] This is setting the bar high, but not impossibly so if the mysteries of the Kingdom are real.

By 'pastoral priests' Bouyer has in mind in the first place what Germans call the *Weltklerus*, the 'secular' clergy of the Latin church. But there are also regular clergy involved in pastoral tasks—not just parochial but in a myriad different settings. There are apostolic Sisters too, in many places, notably in the developing countries, not only the soul but the backbone of the Church-body. We can block these together under the heading 'apostolic religious'.

When it comes to apostolic religious, Bouyer's account is nuanced. On the one hand, in the post-patristic West, new religious orders and congregations tended to replace monastic observance by commitment to service of the neighbour as their members' way of consecration to God. That at any rate would be a standard account of what took place in the emergence of

---

[23] *Ibid.*, pp. 224–5, with an internal citation of I Corinthians 9:22.
[24] Garrigou-Lagrange, *Les trois âges de la vie intérieure*, I, pp. 298–9.

apostolic religious life in Latin Christendom. Considered more deeply, however, the position looks rather different, the departure from patristic-age monasticism less decisive.

> We must recognize in the medieval orders a kind of condensed version of traditional monastic practices, which in many respects renewed them in their reality as well as in their primitive significance. Moreover, with the Jesuits and other modern orders, the essential mortification of the will, proclaimed by all ancient monastic literature as more fundamental than any other ascetic practice, is placed at the very centre of the ascetic effort defined by the vows. Thus it is possible to maintain that these different orders represent equally attempts to acclimatize the spirituality of the desert to the world and to sanctify oneself in the service of men.[25]

What Bouyer terms the 'central spiritual problem' created by the expansion of monasticism into a variety of orders defined by specific missions in the Church is 'the relationship between . . . two aspects: that of personal sanctification by a quasi-monastic existence, and that of personal sanctification in dedication to works of the apostolate or of Christian charity.'[26]

For St Thomas, whom Bouyer quotes with approval, it will not do to say such a life is half-monastic and half-lay, or that it is half-monastic and half-clerical. At least in its Dominican version it is a contemplative life whose apostolic extension consists in communicating to others what one has contemplated. With the addition of some nuances this Dominican understand-

---

[25] Bouyer, *Introduction to Spirituality*, p. 237.
[26] Ibid.

ing, so Bouyer believes, was widely taken up by other apostolic religious: for instance, by Carmelites and Franciscans. It has, he thinks, a secure foundation in the ancient monastic sources, being 'a faithful echo of the most primitive monastic tradition, according to which the most radical anchoritism should normally fructify in a boundless spiritual fatherhood'.[27]

Some modern orders accepted this basic picture while also thinking it possible to 'economize' on traditional monastic observances more than, say, the mediaeval friars had done. All the mediaeval orders of friars were bound not only to the choir office but also to the maintenance of cloister. The trouble comes not so much here as with those more recent religious congregations that reject the very notion of a primacy of contemplation in favour of a primacy of charity. The Jesuits, more distanced from the monks than were the friars, still spoke of being 'contemplative in action'. But in the post-Jesuit period apostolic action can be said to be quite as sanctifying as is contemplation and independently so.

Bouyer will not have it. To set out this choice—apostolic action or contemplation as alternative means to the holiness of charity—is to create a false dilemma. Yes, a 'life of dedication more or less directly apostolic' is 'indisputably very sanctifying', but no, such a life 'cannot be sanctifying if it neglects the interiorizing asceticism developed by monasticism'.[28] Even in the most seemingly secularized apostolic religious life there must be some kind of interiorized monasticism based on a use of ascetic practices of recognizably monastic provenance. Such a life must integrate this

[27] Ibid., p. 238.
[28] Ibid., p. 239.

asceticism if in a form all its own. This is not how modern religious congregation were reformed in the wake of the Second Vatican Council. Bouyer would no doubt say they made a historic mistake, which had repercussions. Observation of Church life aside, Bouyer is only being consistent. If even the asceticism of the married laity is owed in large part to that of monks, as the most basic kind of Christian disciple, we can hardly agree to insulate twenty-first-century members of institutes of consecrated life from the same inspiration.

As elsewhere, we can speak of a plurality of spiritualities corresponding to diverse vocations—but only if we also recognize the significant overlap between spiritualities as between vocations. (Here of course we return to the controversy sparked by the publication of Bouyer's book from which my Preface began.) There are 'common objective elements' in the spiritualities recognized by the Church, and these constitute the 'soul' of 'all authentically Christian spirituality'. Those common objective elements include 'recourse to the fundamental ascetic practices which monastic experience itemized for the first time'.[29] That is why Bouyer can conclude: 'There is no sanctification by means of action alone, but only by action vivified by prayer; and action cannot be thus vivified unless it is marked with the sign of the cross of Christ.'[30]

Appropriately if fortuitously enough, this conclusion looks ahead to the next chapter, which considers the purgative way as the preparation for illumination and the life of union with God.

---

[29] *Ibid.*
[30] *Ibid.*, p. 241.

✣ 6 ✣

Purification

So far I have been discussing the elements of spirituality seen as it were in detachment from their development in any one person's life. On this basis we have covered the Word of God as source, the liturgy as context, the way the Word suitably contextualized generates meditation and contemplation, and the principles of asceticism both common for all and differentiated for groups. I move on now instead to the topic of the dynamic development of spirituality for *the individual over time*.

Using a scheme of venerable antiquity, whose origin is found in Dionysius the Areopagite, the ascetical and mystical way consists of purification, illumination, and union.

Growth and progress?

The sequence of these three terms is undoubtedly meant to suggest a process of growth or progress. It is sometimes questioned whether growth or progress is really an appropriate category to apply to spirituality. The New Testament Scriptures do, however, furnish metaphors of progress in personal sanctification. In his Letter to the Philippians, St Paul declares, 'Forgetting what is behind me, tending toward what is ahead, I run toward the goal, toward the prize of the vocation from on high in Christ Jesus' (3:13). Writing to Corinth, the apostle speaks of new Christians who, having been fed with milk, should move on to more substantial fare (First Corinthians 3:1–2). Writing to Ephesus about the destiny of the whole Church he looks ahead to when its members will form 'a perfect man, to the measure of the mature age of Christ' (4:13). Among the Church Fathers Gregory of Nyssa is an especially strong advocate of the notion of spiritual progress, making good use of Paul's letter to Philippi in this regard.[1] And when expressed less emphatically, that notion could also be regarded as virtually a commonplace of the ancient tradition.

It is where attempts to plot the stages of growth are concerned that a difference of opinion is likely to lie. Both Evagrius and Origen (and notably the first) have in view a series of phases for the ascetical and mystical life. But the version which was spectacularly successful, especially in the West, was that of Dionysius in the celebrated triad we have encountered several times already.

It is important not to treat the Dionysian scheme of purification, illumination, union, in a wooden manner. The kind of distinction being drawn is, rather, 'one of predominant aspects in the spiritual life during one or other of its phases than of rigorously successive forms'.[2] And there is another caveat to enter against taking too literally or exclusively the 'three stages'—or sometimes 'three ages'—of the spiritual life.[3] In

---

[1] Kristina Robb-Dover, 'Gregory of Nyssa's "Perpetual Progress"', *Theology Today* 65. 2 (2008), pp. 213–25.
[2] Bouyer, *Introduction to Spirituality*, p. 245.
[3] Garrigou-Lagrange, *Les trois âges de la vie intérieure*, I, pp. 365–638 (purgative way); II, pp. 3–466 (illuminative way); II,

the league table of holiness, no pundits can predict game-outcomes. While on the one hand, 'there is no peak in the spiritual life here on earth so high that it cannot be transcended', on the other hand 'in certain more or less exceptional cases' God may 'raise a soul from sin to a high degree of sanctity without any very apparent period of transition'.[4] That last observation sets an obvious question-mark against the concept of growth. Yet it also limits its own capacity to subvert that concept by including the phrase 'in certain more or less exceptional cases'.

What is the purgative way?

What, then, is the purgative way, the first of the stages or phases in Dionysius's scheme? Essentially, it is the elimination of our vices with a view to letting the object of faith—the divine mystery in its outreach to us through the Word—take deeper hold on us. It is a tough but salutary warfare where we are sustained by the grace of God but also have to bring our own freedom into full conformity with his grace. The purgative way aims to end the condition of *dipsychia*, the split psyche, spiritual schizophrenia, in which the average human being—including the average baptized human being—lives, so as to establish him or her instead in oneness of heart, which can also be called simplicity of heart or purity of heart.

pp. 467–717 (unitive way). Another influential example is John G. Arintero, OP, *The Mystical Evolution in the Development and Vitality of the Church*. English trans. 2 vols. (Rockford, IL: Tan Books, 1978 [1951]), II, pp. 31–251.

[4] Bouyer, *Introduction to Spirituality*, p. 245.

This comes about when the Spirit of God has supreme reign in us, with the spirit of evil thoroughly vanquished. Holy Baptism has enabled the Spirit of God to take up his dwelling within us, with the spirit of evil exorcized, but the latter uses the 'allies' he still has, both in our flesh and in the world, with a view to reversing the baptismal conversion.[5] This requires on our part an action of 'continually reactivating our faith in the Word', the necessary condition for starting out on the purgative way.[6]

Identifying the vices

On the purgative way it is not enough to recognize that sin is still a vigorous reality in us. We must take account of its different forms, in the light of what Scripture has to say on the topic. This takes some psychological insight. Evagrius was surely endowed with such when he identified 'eight evil thoughts': eight ways of responding to existence that put our lives out of keeping with the divine design for us. His scheme was later tweaked by Gregory the Great to produce in the Latin West the 'seven deadly sins', but I keep here to the Greek eight, the more original version.[7]

How, then, does Evagrius set out his scheme of the eight evil thoughts? Having in mind the Genesis account of the Fall which turns on forbidden fruit, the

---

[5] *Ibid.*, p. 248.
[6] *Ibid.*, p. 249.
[7] I shall follow Bouyer's classic presentation, but a distinctively contemporary slant on Evagrius's scheme can be found in George Tsakiridis, *Evagrius Ponticus and Cognitive Science. A Look at Moral Evil and the Thoughts* (Eugene, OR: Pickwick, 2010).

first he mentions is gluttony. It is the disordered desire for sensuous pleasure in its most rudimentary form. Thence arises the second evil thought, the more serious disorder that is lust. Lust does not affect any merely 'superficial zone' of our sensibility, but its deepest core.[8] To satisfy gluttony and lust, which can be expensive activities, the love of money, thirdly, enters his picture, and this, by its sheer insaneness (why love a medium of exchange?), brings on 'sadness', the fourth evil thought, an incurable dissatisfaction with life. Such sadness, when it fails to make up what is lacking to the self, generates the fifth thought, anger. Then comes lethargy, the sixth evil thought which is not just laziness but a 'growing insensibility to spiritual realities'.[9] Thereafter, seeking for a satisfaction we cannot find in ourselves, we make a display of ourselves even though we are aware of our own lack of substance, and thus fall victim to the seventh thought which is vainglory. Under cover of vainglory, and seeking to conceal our own pettiness, lurks the final evil thought: pride, which, on Evagrius's analysis, is in fact the root sin of the whole process of spiritual rebellion against God.

In the West, Latin mediaeval writers developed a threefold classification of the seven deadly sins, Pope Gregory's modified version of the Evagrian picture. The mediaeval Western analysis corresponds more or less with the areas covered by Evagrius but differs in its tripartite division of vices in terms of lust of the flesh, lust of the eyes, and the pride of life—terms drawn from the First Letter of St John (2:16). The 'lust of the flesh' consists in gluttony, lust and sloth, all three of which ensnare us in pleasure. The 'lust of the eyes'

[8] Bouyer, *Introduction to Spirituality*, p. 249.
[9] Ibid., p. 250.

consists of a single vice, avarice, or attachment to the riches real or apparent that others have rather than the attachment we ought to have, which is to our true good. The 'pride of life', like the lust of the flesh, is threefold. It consists of the pride that makes us the centre of everything, the envy of rivals that follows from this and the anger that results from envy when it is frustrated. These schemes, Eastern and Western, should not be thought of as exhaustive. They do, however, help us to gain a realistic awareness of the concrete reality of sin in our lives.

Growing in the virtues

I said that the purgative way entails the extirpation of vices so that the object of faith can take deeper hold on us. The renewal of baptismal faith, when we renounced sin and accepted God's offer of salvation in Jesus Christ, is, then, the basic departure point of the *via purgativa*, reinvigorating as it does the impetus of faith in our life. It is not enough to provide a phenomenology of the vices. We also need a narrative of how they may be shaken off, and it begins here, in the waters, in the 'sacrament of faith'.

In the collection of Byzantine ascetical and mystical texts called the *Philokalia* (it covers a thousand years of authors, from the fourth century to the fifteenth), faith is the starting-point of a set of 'Directions to Hesychasts', i.e. advice for those aspiring to *hēsykhia*, the inner peace of contemplation. These 'Directions' are ascribed to two canonized monastics from the end of the period covered by the *Philokalia*, St Callistus and St Ignatius. In the 'Directions', the basic act of Christian faith is what sets in motion all growth in holiness, starting with the purgative way. Callistus and Ignatius wrote, 'The beginning of every action pleasing to God is calling with faith on the life-saving name of our Lord Jesus Christ, as He Himself said, "Without me ye can do nothing" (John 15:5)'.[10] The same Johannine text, from Jesus's discourse on the Vine and the Branches, is cited again as Callistus and Ignatius continue: 'The [beginners on the purgative way] should invoke His [i.e. Jesus's] holy and most sweet name, bearing it always in the mind, in the heart and on the lips. They should force themselves in every possible way to live, breathe, sleep and wake, walk, eat and drink with Him and in Him, and in general so to do all that they have to do. For as in His absence all harmful things come to us, leaving no room for anything to profit the soul, so in His presence all evil is swept away, no good is ever lacking and everything becomes possible, as the Lord Himself says, "He that abideth in me, and I in him, the same bringeth forth much fruit; for without me ye can do nothing" (John 15:5)'.[11]

But why is the act of faith, expressed here in the invocation of the Holy Name of Jesus, the beginning of the purgative way? On the classic analysis offered by, say, St Thomas, faith involves both the intellect and the will. It is, as they say, an intellectual-voluntary synthesis, where both mind and heart are engaged, the mind opening itself to God as Truth itself, the heart or will to God as Goodness itself. As such, the act of

---

[10] Callistus and Ignatius, *Directions to Hesychasts*, 8, in E. Kadloubovsky and G. E. H. Palmer (tr.), *Writings from the Philokalia on Prayer of the Heart* (London: Faber and Faber, 1951), p. 169.

[11] Callistus and Ignatius, *Directions to Hesychasts*, 13, in Kadloubovsky and Palmer, *Writings from the Philokalia on Prayer of the Heart*, p. 173.

faith is what is needed to counteract our own fall into the unnatural passions, which was also an intellectual-voluntary act, of a catastrophic kind. Such a fall, ratifying the Fall of the proto-parents, begins by the emergence in our consciousness of some sinful desire. The thought of sin, if we relish it, delight in it, couples what is passing through our minds with the intentions of the evil angels in the warfare they wage against our spiritual good. The thought, the intellectual element, then becomes ripe for union with a voluntary element: namely, the consent of our will to what our thought entertains. When that happens, the inner unnatural passion is duly produced, assisted by appropriate mental images which remain in the memory when the disordered feeling has passed.

In the struggle against sin, Callistus and Ignatius recommend the continual calling to mind of the Name of Jesus as a concentrated way of renewing the act of faith, a way which, just because it is so simple, is possible in all circumstances. This lies behind the use of the Jesus Prayer in the Byzantine and Slavonic East, a practice which, sometimes making use of an Orthodox prayer-rope (a so-called 'Orthodox rosary'), has also spread into the modern West. But whether or not one decides to accept this advice and make use of the Prayer of the Name, the basic faith-attitude of prayerful dependence on God in Jesus Christ still has to be developed in some form if the purgative way is to be undertaken at all.

Continuing on that way, faith can be expected to stimulate growth by means of the virtues, thinking here of the virtues that spring precisely from the act of faith. Callistus and Ignatius mention first of all in this connexion peace and love. Staniloae was the translator into Romanian of the *Philokalia* where their texts appear. He also amplified its textual resources from a thorough-going knowledge of the spiritual tradition of the Fathers, and provided the anthology with ample introductions and notes. Unlike Callistus and Ignatius, Staniloae's rendition of 'philokalic' spirituality has in mind not simply devout Christians seeking perfection as contemplatives but *all* Christians, including those just starting to slough off lives of really hardened sin. That is why, in his narrative of purification, appeal is made to the earlier ascetic writers—beginning with Evagrius—who place first among the fruits of faith the fear of God, a fear made especially acute by the thought of judgment. I shall be following him.

The fear in question is not the loving fear we tend to hear about in modern sermons. Nor is it a fear of missing out on divine blessing. It is, frankly, what St Thomas would call the 'servile' fear which wants to escape the punishments of God. This may not be so exalted as the 'filial' fear praised by Aquinas, but it is a useful fear nonetheless. It enables us to counteract what Staniloae calls the 'fear of the world' in us.[12] By this phrase he means fear of the hardships the world can inflict on us, a fear which drives us heedlessly to chase the world's pleasures and prosperity while they are still available—at all costs not to let the world get the better of us in the struggle for survival. Fear of the world, so understood, dominates much human life. The usefulness of the fear of God lies in its power to counter such 'fear of the world' by promoting a salutary awareness: if we seek to turn the world from enemy to friend, we may lose out on our ultimate intended destiny. The world as known since the Fall,

---

[12] Staniloae, *Orthodox Spirituality*, p. 132.

the world organized without God and even against God, is 'a danger to our true and eternal existence'.[13]

Thus the ascetic tradition invites us to meditate on the thought of our last judgment, the immediate or personal judgment that will follow biological death. In the East, the popular spiritual treatise called *The Ladder* by St John Climacus has a good deal of material on this, and it is paralleled by the *bona mors* ('good death') spiritual exercises of the mediaeval and early modern West.

On the basis of the fear of God, as generated by faith, the ascetic tradition expects to experience repentance: repentance for our past condition and the acts in which that condition found expression. This repentance will be expressed in watchfulness, taking care that the delinquencies of the past are not repeated in the present and the future. Repentance is a key motif of the purgative way. For St Isaac the Syrian, a seventh-century writer quoted in the *Directions to Hesychasts* by Callistus and Ignatius, 'repentance is a second grace [after Baptism] and is born in the heart from faith and fear'.[14] This reference to the first grace, Baptismal grace, may remind us of the liturgical context of spirituality which we considered in Chapter 2. As if taking up this cue, Staniloae writes: 'The work of purification is realized by the powers which flow from the Mysteries of Baptism and Repentance [i.e. the sacraments of Baptism and Penance], just as illumination is an actualization of the powers given by the mystery

---

[13] *Ibid.*
[14] Callistus and Ignatius, *Directions to Hesychasts*, 80, in Kadloubovsky and Palmer, *Writings from the Philokalia on Prayer of the Heart*, p. 248.

of Chrism,[i.e. the sacrament of Confirmation] while union with God is an effect of the Eucharist.'[15]

When the passions have obstructed the progress of baptismal grace, the grace of repentance—whether in the sacrament of Penance or through the activity of repentance—sets obstacles aside, so as to free a way for the grace of Baptism again. In the ancient Eastern ascetic tradition such repentance comprises three elements: prayer for forgiveness, observation of thoughts, and the endurance of troubles.

The first element in repentance, then, is the most obvious one, *prayer for forgiveness*. Harping on the need for forgiveness may seem negative but repentance is not meant to induce discouragement. On the contrary, as Staniloae points out, discouragement is logically 'opposed to repentance, because where something better can't be expected, regret has no place'.[16] Repentance judges the past with the conviction that, thanks to divine power, the self can do better in present and future. Though relentless in distrust of our present state, it is filled with trust in divine possibilities for the future. Such repentance tends to undermine egoism. Be the passions fleshly or psychic, they are all heads of the same self-obsessed dragon. We make looking back a force for the future by a decision not to repeat the past, to move from the kingdom of egoism into the kingdom of love. By such ongoing repentance we prepare ourselves for the sacrament of Repentance just as by the sacrament of Repentance this state or condition or habit of repentance is itself stimulated and sustained. Without the praying for forgiveness that belongs with such habitual repentance we may well

---

[15] Staniloae, *Orthodox Spirituality*, p. 135.
[16] Ibid., p. 139.

forget the sinful words, thoughts and deeds we should bring to the sacrament, while without the sacrament we might be unaware of how our deliverance from sin involves the Mystical Body which we have harmed. In the sacrament we are also given the opportunity to hear from the priest an objective judgment which, hopefully is, neither too merciful nor too condemning as our own self-judgement can often be. In the Eastern tradition if not only there, such repentance is associated with a gift of tears that wash the heart and make it transparent to the self.

We come now to the second element in repentance as found in the *Philokalia*: the *observation of thoughts* or 'guarding of the mind'. The guarding of the mind (also called 'watchfulness' or 'vigilance') is directed not only to rejecting evil thoughts but also to welcoming good ones and associating them with movement towards God. For a good thought can be waylaid by an evil one, as in an example given by Evagrius: 'I have the thought to offer hospitality and truly for the Lord, but the tempter comes—he cuts it off and puts in the soul the thought to do it for [vain]glory'.[17] In his treatise on Baptism Mark the Monk advises that the best antidote to the tricks the mind plays is to take any good thought that comes to us and offer it immediately to the Lord as a sacrifice, on the model of the offerings of first fruits in the Old Testament. The guarding of thoughts thus becomes 'a continual recital of the name of God in the mind'.[18]

I said that in the *Philokalia* tradition, as interpreted by Staniloae, repentance typically comprises prayer for forgiveness, observation of thoughts, and endurance

---

[17] Cited *ibid.*, p. 161.
[18] *Ibid.*, p. 167.

of troubles. There remains then of this trio *endurance of troubles*, namely: longsuffering in the patient enduring of trials. Patience in the face of the trials that others cause us, or troubles coming at us from other sources, undermines the passion of anger and contributes to a further weakening of the movements of appetite. Moreover, the soul that, by self-restraint, has made progress with the disordered passions of gluttony, lust and avarice may be tempted by vainglory and pride at the thought of its own spiritual success. In that situation, trials and tribulations constitute a helpful divine pedagogy. Such trials can be 'felt as a kind of forsaking by God' but in reality they are no such thing.[19] And Staniloae invokes here, appropriately enough, the idea of 'passive purification' as discussed by the sixteenth-century Spanish Carmelite doctor John of the Cross.[20]

This brings us to the next emergent virtue in Stanilaoe's synthesis of the *Philokalia* tradition. After fear of God and repentance comes hope. In Staniloae's words, hope is faith 'oriented to the future', certitude about participation in the eschatological realities in the Age to Come.'[21] In his Commentary on the First Letter to Timothy, St Thomas remarks pithily, 'Faith shows the end, hope makes us tend toward it, charity realizes union with it'.[22] In his *Compendium theologiae*, Thomas says of God that he 'lifts up a wave of hope in the believer's heart, to receive with the help of faith those goods that he naturally desires and that hope

---

[19] *Ibid.*, p. 169.
[20] *Ibid.*, p. 171.
[21] *Ibid.*, p. 177.
[22] Thomas Aquinas, *Commentary on the First Letter of Timothy*, 1, I.5.

makes him know'.[23] 'Naturally desires', because—so one of Thomas's finest expositors explains—a natural desire for the completion of one's being can 'become a true desire for beatitude under the enlightenment and motion of grace, and finally identified with the only living and true God.'[24] For Aquinas, beatitude is the 'first and main object of all prayer'.[25]

From the patient endurance of troubles, sustained with the virtue of hope for our true goal, there issue two more virtues, closely inter-related with each other: 'meekness' and 'humility'. Meekness comes from the elimination of anger. Born as it is of patience together with hope, it proves resistant to disappointments of all kinds. It also paves the way for humility. If the passions cause all things to be viewed egoistically then humility, the converse of egoism, re-establishes a true understanding of reality. As Staniloae puts it: 'Humility looks like self-reduction to nothing; in reality it is a return of our nature to the place where it is a window [on] the infinite and [an] empty room intended to be filled with divine light.'[26]

And so finally we arrive at *apatheia*, the dispassionate state, the strength of which is the power of all the virtues put together. Despite its negative name ('passionlessness'), *apatheia* is essentially positive. It is the liberation of the spirit and a complete mastery of self, so that the self may be for God. In principle it can be lost, for human beings are temporal and mutable. They are not angels for whom the life of goodness is either achieved or negated in a single moment. Yet the loss

---

[23] Thomas Aquinas, *Compendium theologiae*, II. 1.
[24] Torrell, *Saint Thomas Aquinas*, vol. 2, *Spiritual Master*, p. 327.
[25] *Ibid.*, p. 331, note 67.
[26] Staniloae, *Orthodox Spirituality*, p. 184.

of *apatheia* is morally improbable. Though, to be sure, *apatheia* requires sustaining by the will, nevertheless it is by definition the overcoming of the passions and the establishment of all the virtues so far mentioned in their unity. What distinguishes the idea of *apatheia* from that of the virtues which compose it? Unlike the virtues, *apatheia* is essentially a state, and specifically a state of quiet or peace, the state of realized—even if not final or ultimate—*hēsykhia*. It is characterized by the gathering up of all our powers, whether of soul and body, in positive relation to God.

With *apatheia* charity—*agapē*—can appear fully for the first time, for egoism has met with resounding defeat. *Apatheia* is the real possibility of the dominance of life by the kind of love that charity is. 'Dispassion [a synonym for *apatheia*] is tranquillity', remarks Staniloae, 'because the gentle breeze of love is blowing'.[27] This is what makes *apatheia* the preliminary condition for contemplation, and especially for supernatural contemplation.

By *apatheia* the soul enters a stable condition of not being subject to the flesh and the world. Instead the soul is subject instead to the Spirit of God, as was intended by the Creator at the beginning. *Apatheia* disposes the heart for the infusion of charity to the highest degree, thanks to the coming of that Spirit with renewed power. By permitting adherence to charity with no sense of inner constraint, *apatheia* draws us more fully into the life of the Kingdom.

It is I think evident that what Staniloae has described, on the basis of the *Philokalia* tradition, is what the New Testament calls *metanoia*, change of the *nous*, the deep mind or spirit, alias conversion. Faith, moved from

---

[27] Ibid., p. 190.

within by charity, now begins to be fully alive. This is what the redeeming action of God has been aiming at from the beginning, the bud that is our initial 'justification' by grace really flowering, and showing its true colours. I have already cited St Thomas on how charity enables actual union with the end—the *End*, God himself as man's beatitude—which faith first allows us to know. In a fuller statement by him: 'Charity signifies not only the love of God, but also a certain friendship with him; which implies, besides love, a certain mutual return of love, together with a certain mutual communion'.[28] We can easily see how *apatheia* could find its place in St Thomas's itinerary of the way to God. It helps charity to grow by letting it really take root in the human subject who has received it. And once charity has bedded in, all the other virtues come into play.[29]

The terminus

The terminus of the purgative way, where it transmutes into first the illuminative and then the unitive way, is more difficult to ascertain. Just as we cannot date the beginning of the human desire for union with God, so we cannot date the point when the process of purgation is complete. Evagrius, though, suggests some recognizable signs of an effective purification of the soul. One is the possibility of praying without distractions. Another is the way the soul is no longer subject to the attractions of the world, including those attractions

---

[28] Thomas Aquinas, *Summa theologiae*, Ia. IIae., q. 65, a. 5. 'Communion' here translates the Latin *societas* in the light of the term common to both Aristotle and the Greek Bible, *koinonia*.

[29] *Ibid.*, IIa. IIae., q. 23, a. 8, ad iii.

that are not actually present to us but only present in memory and imagination. A third sign, stressed by the fifth-century St John Cassian who brought much of the Desert tradition, including Evagrius's contribution, to the West, concerns the nature of our dreams. Purity of soul may be expected to manifest itself in subconscious life as well as in conscious existence. For another John, St John of the Cross, the process of purification must take place not just once but often. 'First applied to the senses, it must be continued in the most interior, the most spiritual aspects of the soul, and it will not be completed until the soul is immersed in God, and at the resurrection, its very body [likewise].'[30] There is a journey by which 'beginners' on the road of charity become 'proficient' and ultimately 'perfect',[31] but it is not without its unexpected twists and turns.

---

[30] A paraphrase of sanjuanist teaching in Bouyer, *Introduction to Spirituality*, p. 259.
[31] Thomas Aquinas, *Summa theologiae*, IIa. IIae., q. 24, a. 9.

✢ 7 ✢

Illumination

T O SOME EXTENT what has already been said about purification indicates the place of illumination, or the illuminative way.

Fuller presence, greater love, more knowledge

If the purgative way runs its course as it should, then the disordered 'impressions' that have hitherto carried us away lose their dominance. We are freed to make further progress in loving God—the God who, thanks to *apatheia*'s openness to *agapē*, can be present to us that much more effectively. This more powerful presence to us of God himself on the illuminative way would seem to be what is most emphasized in the Greek-speaking East.

The Latin tradition stresses how, once the purgative way has run its course, Christian doctrine becomes more alive for us. Truths of faith, formerly foreign to our experience, and to that extent obscure, now become luminous and genuinely enlighten us. The propositional truths offered to us for our belief on the basis of Scripture and Tradition cease to be looked at from the outside and become instead (as it were) something to be inhabited, to be lived in. The faith without which the *via purgativa* could never have commenced, begins to be a knowing faith.

That emphasis is not alien to the patristic East. As illumination dawns, faith starts to be characterized by what the Greeks call *gnosis* — appealing of course to the orthodox not the pagan sense of that controversial word. Faith is starting to have some foretaste of the object of the act of faith — God as beatifying us by his saving work in Christ, the full experience of which will not be available, however, until the Age to Come. I shall come back to the terminology of *gnosis* later.

But since the illuminative way depends for its possibility not on any intellectual development but on the elimination of the vices in the *via purgativa*, this second stage of the mystical path is intimately bound up with continuing advance in the virtues. *Apatheia*, so we saw in the last chapter, has let us give ourselves over to *agape*, to the love of God. To the illuminative way there corresponds, then, 'a flowering within us of charity illuminating our whole being, in such a way that faith in God Who is Himself charity, finally enlightens an intelligence attuned to know Him.'[1]

Charity assimilates us to the God who is Love. So by means of *connaturalitas* ('connaturality'), the word used by St Thomas — maybe 'sympathy' is the best we can do in ordinary English — charity-love inclines us to understand better what God has revealed, because what God has revealed is precisely that he *is* Love and his plan is love too. Charity also branches out to affect the development of a range of virtues, growth in which corresponds to the gradual restoration of our nature, as made in the image of God, made to God's likeness. This is not only a matter of faith, hope and charity, the supernatural theological virtues. There are also, at any rate for St Thomas, supernaturalized

---

[1] Bouyer, *Introduction to Spirituality*, p. 262.

versions of the moral virtues coming about in us with the infusion of charity. Fortitude, justice, and temperance gain 'a depth, a fullness of meaning and reality that the ancients never even suspected',[2] reshaped as they can be by love. For example, pagans would never have guessed that one day the virtue of fortitude would include readiness for martyrdom. On the illuminative way, then, come both an enhancement of enhanced knowledge and an increase in charity. Enhanced knowledge, increased charity, these are the twin marks of the second stage of the spiritual life, of the ascetical and mystical ascent to God.

Divine friendship is developing *from both sides*, God and man—and what friendship can be without mutuality? St Thomas remarks on this in his *Summa contra Gentiles*, drawing in one of his—and St Augustine's—favoured sources on this topic, the First Letter of St John. 'It is manifest that God loves to the highest degree those whom he has made his friends by the Holy Spirit, only so great a love could confer such a good ... Now, since every beloved being lives in him who loves it, it is therefore necessary that through the Holy Spirit not only does God live in us, but we too live in God.'[3]

Kataphasis and *apophasis* in the spiritual life

I referred to 'enhanced knowledge': some would challenge that phrase. The claim has been made that such concern with knowledge is essentially Hellenic, a borrowing from pagan culture, rather than Hebraic and

---

[2] Ibid., p. 264.
[3] Thomas Aquinas, *Summa contra Gentiles*, IV, 21.

thus authentically biblical. Put in terms of this simplistic contrast, the objection does not seem well-founded. Using at times some Greek philosophical notions in an instrumental way, Christianity refashioned a theme which, in itself, is perfectly biblical: the theme, namely, of the knowledge of God enjoyed by the prophets and communicated by them to Israel. This is the intimate knowledge of God compared in the Hebrew Bible compares to the union of man and wife in marriage.

As we shall see, there *is* a role for 'unknowing'—for learned ignorance—on the mystical way. But it does not eliminate the role of enhanced knowledge. Over against the apophatic—what goes beyond speech, there stands the cataphatic—what can be expressed in speech. For the Bible, that will mean what is expressed in divine speech, the speech of the Word as made known to human beings, and never more so than when the speech in question contributes to the making of Covenant-relationship.

For Israel, religious knowledge belongs essentially with the Covenant. In the extraordinary Covenant-creating events of Exodus and Sinai, God 'had taken the initiative in establishing a close relationship between himself and his people',[4] without prejudice, however, to the continuing distance between them which the Lordship of God inevitably entails. In the encounter between Moses and the Lord on the mountain-top (Exodus 33:17–23), justice is done to the apophatic for 'God himself remains hidden from sight even though he makes enough of himself known to confirm the reality of his active presence'.[5] 'Makes enough of himself

---

[4] Bernhard W. Anderson, *The Living World of the Old Testament* (London: Longmans, Green and Co., 1966, 2nd edition), p. 64.
[5] *Ibid.*, p. 65.

known' for, as the exegete Bernhard Anderson, here cited, goes on: 'Israel believed firmly that God was also near and that he had invited them into a covenant relationship.'[6] And, unfolding this second, cataphatic, dimension of the Covenant, Anderson continues: 'On the human side such knowledge has two aspects. On the one hand, this is a *theological* knowledge which can be taught by parents in the home (Deuteronomy 6:20–5) or by cultic officials at the sanctuaries, especially at the covenant-renewal festivals. It is the knowledge of who God is (Hosea 13:4), what he has done for Israel, and what he requires of his people—in short, a knowledge of the covenant tradition ... On the other hand, this is a knowledge which includes the *will* as well as the mind. Hosea [just cited] was talking about the knowledge of the heart—that is, the response of the *whole person* to God's love.'[7]

In his *Life of Moses*, a spiritual theology set deliberately against the Old Testament background, the fourth-century Cappadocian father St Gregory of Nyssa associates the beginning of the illuminative way with a particular episode in the Book of Exodus. It is the episode where Moses sees at the foot of Mount Sinai a bush that burns yet is not consumed, whereupon he takes off his shoes, recognizing he is in the presence of the Holy, of the Fire of God himself (Exodus 3:2–6). In Gregory's understanding of the cataphatic, there is here a movement into light, as the darkness—in Greek, *skotos*—of error is dispelled by the light of truth, in a process at once intellectual and moral. For the soul in this Moses-like condition there comes about, in Andrew Louth's words, a 'recognition

---

[6] *Ibid.*
[7] *Ibid.*, p. 249.

that God alone truly exists, that he is the only worthy object of the soul's love'.[8] Accordingly, Lev Gillet, the French Orthodox priest who wrote under the pseudonym 'A Monk of the Eastern Church', understood the epiphany to Moses as a disclosure not only of being ('I am who Am', Exodus 3:14) but of self-gift—which is another name for love. 'The Being I am is a Being of fire . . . My fire does not destroy . . . And my flame has no need to be fed. It imparts itself, gives itself. I am the Gift that never ceases to give itself.'[9] This reading of the epiphany at Horeb suits well the transition moment from the purgative to the illuminative way. As Louth remarks, 'the purified soul does not simply learn the vanity of all created things but also learns to see in them a manifestation of the glory of God'.[10]

Thereafter in Gregory's *Life of Moses*, the progressive movement enters a darkness of a different kind from the darkness of error. Significantly, Gregory chooses here a quite distinct word for 'the dark': not *skotos* but *gnophos*, following the cue given by the Moses story in its Septuagint version. 'Moses went into the dark cloud where God was (Exodus 20:21).' 'The dark cloud': this includes, within the Exodus narrative, both the 'cloud' Moses entered during his first ascent up the mountain, and also the 'thick darkness' in which, on his second ascent, he became enveloped. In Nyssa's *Life of Moses*, the darkness in question 'does not at all mean that God is remote from the soul and can never be attained. On the contrary, in the darkness God is present to the soul,

---

[8] Louth, *The Origins of the Christian Mystical Tradition*, p. 84.
[9] Lev Gillet, *The Burning Bush* (Oxford: Fellowship of Saint Alban and Saint Sergius, 1976; Springfield, IL: Templegate, n. d.), p. 17.
[10] Louth, *The Origins of the Christian Mystical Tradition*, p. 85.

and the soul is united with him'.[11] This is the apophatic experience, as made possible by the illuminative way. Some critics complain. The adjective 'apophatic' cannot qualify the noun 'experience' without cancelling it out. They are right insofar as here unknowability is joined with knowledge. In Stanilaoe's words, 'In the measure in which we ascend toward the divine mystery, we are filled with more and more knowledge—of course with another kind of knowledge, but also with the knowledge that the divine nature is above all knowledge.'[12]

That is not quite the position of the best known English representative of apophaticism, the fourteenth-century author of *The Cloud of Unknowing*. For the Cloud author, not a combination of knowing and unknowing, but only what he calls 'longing love' can make spiritual use of the darkness of God. In what are probably the most often cited lines from his treatise he tells his readers: 'And therefore shape thee to bide in this darkness as long as thou mayest, evermore crying after him whom thou lovest. For if ever thou shall see him or feel him as it may be here, it must always be in this cloud and in this darkness ... Smite upon that thick cloud of unknowing with a sharp dart of longing love.'[13] The Cloud author is reading his Greek sources, essentially Dionysius, through the lens of the 'love mysticism' which would increasingly dominate the Western Middle Ages.

Yet on either view—whether the more cognitively optimistic one in Staniloae or the less cognitively optimistic in the mediaeval English author—the divine incomprehensibility does not slam the entrance door

---

[11] Ibid., p. 90.
[12] Staniloae, *Orthodox Spirituality*, pp. 235–6.
[13] Cited in Knowles, *The English Mystical Tradition*, p. 77.

to the *via illuminativa*. Rather, the incomprehensibility of God is an invitation to continue going forward on that way. The longing of the soul for God is divinely sustained in an intimate fashion as the soul's sense of God's presence grows in strength. In this it is assisted by all the virtues that pertain to the condition of *apatheia* as won on the *via purgativa* as that condition opens the soul efficaciously to love.

Conformation and knowledge

We have already encountered the notion of assimilation by 'connaturality', by sympathetic attunement to another reality—specifically, charity-love as assimilating us to the God who in his revelation shows us he is a God of Love, and that his plan is a plan of love. 'Assimilation' and 'conformation' are well-nigh identical terms. The theme of 'conformation'—meaning, conformation to what is made known on the illuminative way—is essential to the ultimate 'union' to which the illuminative way tends. 'Because the People of God is the People that knows Him, its members must become like Him,' remarks Bouyer.[14] In other words, they must become *conformed* to him, and in this way *united more closely* to him. In the Old Testament's so-called 'Holiness Code' we read, 'Be holy as I am holy' (Leviticus 20:7). And this is echoed at the close of the Sermon on the Mount in the words of Jesus, 'Be perfect as your heavenly Father is perfect' (Matthew 5:48). Here the point of the Covenant knowledge of God is to bring about resemblance to God, a resemblance which will lead to conformation, to sharing a 'form'.

[14] Bouyer, *Introduction to Spirituality*, p. 265.

In keeping with the Old Testament revelation of the Word, Bouyer speaks of how the antecedent knowledge God has of us makes possible our knowledge of him. This knowledge on God's part is not the same as his general knowledge of creation as a consequence of the omniscience which belongs to his Essence. God's knowledge of each of his chosen ones is not simply a knowledge that registers facts. It is an elective knowledge whereby God knows us in love, in our individual particularity, with a view to bringing us to himself. But if, in St Paul's words, I am, 'to know even as I am known' (I Corinthians 13:12), then my knowledge of God must become a loving knowledge of him just as his knowledge is a loving knowledge of me. Otherwise the reciprocity in question (to 'know even as I am known') will be impossible.

This love-factor is vital to the distinctively biblical approach to *gnosis*. Many people would shun the term 'gnosis' in the context of spiritual theology, fearing its non-Christian associations. In our own contemporary period, when Gnostic texts are eagerly studied in order to present a view of Christian origins incompatible with that of the Church, the associations of the word are often anti-ecclesial in character. But on the illuminative way we pass, as its name implies, from simple faith to gnosis, which must always be distinguished from the *'pseudo-gnosis'*, or *'gnosis* falsely so called' of Gnosticism, famously denounced by such Fathers of the Church as St Irenaeus.[15]

If we are alarmed by use of the word 'gnosis', Greek-speaking Jews and the New Testament writers

---

[15] Hans Urs von Balthasar, *The Scandal of the Incarnation. Irenaeus Against the Heresies*. English trans. (San Francisco: Ignatius, 1990).

were not. In the Septuagint, the Alexandrian translation of the Old Testament, 'gnosis' stands for precisely the kind of knowledge of God found in the prophets. The Alexandrian Jew Philo of Alexandria began to use this same terminology, in dependence on the biblical texts, for all salutary knowledge, all knowledge pertinent to salvation. In the Synoptic Gospels we hear of a *gnosis* of the mysteries of the Kingdom, transmitted under the veil of parables (Matthew 13:11 with a Lucan parallel). A logion in the Synoptic tradition concentrates this same *gnosis* on the person of the Son. 'No one knows the Father but the Son, and anyone to whom the Son chooses to reveal him'. (Matthew 11:27 with a Lucan parallel). Thanks to revelation, the Son is known by Jesus's disciples with a kind of knowing that participates in the Father's own knowledge of him. For St Paul such *gnosis*, the *gnosis* of the mystery of Christ, is a gift of the Spirit characteristic of the last stage in God's plan. Paul uses the phrase 'the *gnosis* of the mystery' (Ephesians 3:4) to encourage his readers to discover in Christ himself all 'the treasures of the wisdom of God' (Colossians 2:3). The other outstanding New Testament theologian, St John, does not use the noun *gnosis*, only the verbal form, *gnomai*, but, as von Balthasar has pointed out, John never sets believing over against knowing, as some later writers would do. Rather, for John, believing brings knowing in its train. 'To know' Christ is the realization of living faith.[16] The state of grace—a reality for all those justified by Baptism and recovered, where sin intrudes, by repentance on the purgative way, is nothing less than the 'habitual

---

[16] Hans Urs von Balthasar, *The Glory of the Lord. A Theological Aesthetics I. Seeing the Form*. English trans. (Edinburgh: T. & T. Clark, 1982), p. 141.

possibility of living an experiential knowledge of the divine Persons'.[17] In *gnosis*—Aquinas would write *experimentalis cognitio*—the possible becomes actual. The indwelling of the Holy Trinity is the true foundation for such knowing God.

The knowledge which comes about on the illuminative way may be summed up as the increasingly contemplative orientation that meditation on the divine Word now takes. That will mean a real and efficacious, and no longer simply notional or formal, apprehension of the truths of faith, and the unification of those truths in an ever more simple and profound view of the mystery of God in Christ, a view lovingly assimilated by us, perfecting our adoptive sonship of the Father and setting up 'an interchange between the knowledge that [already] conforms us to Him Whom we know, and that more perfect conformity which causes us to know Him [even] more intimately ', and ever more intimately if we continue to make progress.[18]

This mature Christian gnostic awareness, achieved as the illuminative way comes to its climax, is also the stage at which knowledge of the divine outreach to us—what the Greek East calls the 'divine energies'[19]— must necessarily be accompanied by apophasis in its fulness. Here is where the message of the *Cloud* author comes into its own. There has always been an element of the apophatic on the illuminative way because the apophatic is an inherent dimension of the covenant relationship. At the close of the illuminative way, what

[17] Albert Patfoort, OP, 'Mission divines et expérience des personnes divines selon S. Thomas', *Angelicum* 63 (1986), pp. 545–59, and here at p. 552.
[18] Bouyer, *Introduction to Spirituality*, p. 275.
[19] A classic starting point is St Basil's writings *Against Eunomius*, especially I.6; II.4; II.32.

prevails, as in the life of Moses, is the darkness of God. It is not the highest possible prayer; that would require the experience of the Uncreated Light, with its consequences in what in the West the Carmelite teachers call the 'spiritual marriage' and the 'transforming union' and these are proper to the unitive way where the soul is filled with light. The apophatic state eventuates, in Staniloae's words, 'before the holy light comes to it'.[20] But it is nonetheless prayer of a very high order, entailing a total quietness (*hēsykhia*) of the mind in a darkness where the presence of God is more keenly felt than it has ever been before.

Pure prayer

It is now that prayer becomes not just simpler but more absorbing. Now what the soul finds is that 'When [it] fixes its thought on a word of Scripture, on a particular mystery, or on the mystery of Christ in the fullness and unity that attract it more and more, it is simply absorbed therein'.[21] At this point, God's own mastery of the soul through its belonging to Christ becomes, under the movement of the Spirit, almost palpable. In the language invented by St Teresa of Avila, we are moving from the prayer of recollection and the prayer of simple regard to the *prayer of quiet* defined as a prayer 'in which the activity of God in us seems to absorb our own'.[22] As St John of the Cross puts it, 'When it comes to pass that the soul is conscious of being led into silence, and hearkens, it must forget

---

[20] Staniloae, *Orthodox Spirituality*, p. 239.
[21] Bouyer, *Introduction to Spirituality*, p. 275.
[22] *Ibid.*, p. 276.

even the practice of that loving advertence of which I have spoken, so that it may remain free for that which the Lord then desires of it'.[23]

For the writers anthologized in the *Philokalia*, the mind now sinks down into the heart, forming few words, among which, however, should always be the Name of Jesus. This is unconsciously echoed by the fourteenth-century English hermit-mystic Richard Rolle who says of the gift of contemplation, 'no one will receive it, unless he love specially the name of Jesus and honour it so that he never allow it to fall from his memory save in sleep'.[24] The Jesus Prayer represents a very modest amplification of this counsel since the text runs 'Lord Jesus Christ Son of God have mercy on me' or, in some uses, 'have mercy on us'. We have already looked at the function of the Jesus Prayer on the purgative way where its task is to separate us from evil thoughts. The role of this prayer in 'pure' prayer is different, however, as Staniloae explains. 'If the mind can give up images and concepts, it can't give up in general every kind of activity and feeling, except for a few moments of silence or of interior rapture, reached at the height of prayer. So if the mind's exits are closed and it is forced to return to its center, "to the heart", it must be given another content; in other words that one content in which we want [the mind] to gather [its activities together].'[25] Penetrating into the heart, this prayer finds the Jesus who has been in us 'trans-consciously' (Staniloae finds that a better term than sub-consciously) ever since our Baptism. Here

---

[23] St John of the Cross, *The Living Flame of Love*, III. 35.
[24] Richard Rolle, *The Fire of Love*, XV.
[25] Staniloae, *Orthodox Spirituality*, pp. 257–8.

the Jesus Prayer comes into its own at a level of depth previously unknown.[26]

In the Byzantine tradition such pure prayer is seen as helped by certain tips about posture (preferably the one practising the prayer of quiet should be seated, his eyes fixed on the chest, the seat of the physical heart) and breathing in a slow and regular manner. In the version of such prayer found in the anonymous mid-nineteenth-century Russian work *The Way of a Pilgrim*, each heart-beat is synchronized with one word of the Jesus Prayer.[27]

Now the mind becomes transparent to an unlimited content, which Staniloae expresses as follows: 'The humility of prayer grows from the simultaneous consciousness of our subject [i.e. myself] and of the supreme Subject [i.e. God], distinct from each other, but in relationship and reciprocal penetration.'[28]

Reciprocal, yet God is here the principal Subject and our subject stands in his shadow. We experience him as the primary Subject to the point that he fills our subjectivity and we forget ourselves. If it can still be called prayer (and the question might be raised), it is prayer in a silence overwhelmed by amazement. After this there is nothing more man can do by effort, even effort under grace. In his book *The English Mystical Tradition* David Knowles wrote: 'The truly mystical initial prayer is distinguished...by an awareness of a love and knowledge and "presence" of God that does not proceed from any thought or conscious motive,

---

[26] Now the soul 'begins to use the great treasures there', *ibid.*, p. 259.
[27] R. M. French (tr.), *The Way of a Pilgrim, and The Pilgrim Continues his Way* (San Francisco: Harper, 1991).
[28] Staniloae, *Orthodox Spirituality*, p. 291.

but is in the soul without the previous activity of its faculties.'[29]

Only a fuller coming of the Holy Spirit to raise the mind to the vision of the divine Light can allow the soul to go further than this already extraordinary condition. If the Holy Spirit visits us in that manner, then transition from the illuminative way to the unitive way comes about.

---

[29] Knowles, *The English Mystical Tradition*, p. 19.

✧ 8 ✧

Union

For obvious reasons, the unitive way is the most difficult part of spirituality to speak or write about. Those on the way of union are not just enlightened, as on the illuminative way. More than that, they are lost in light.

The experience of union

'Pure prayer has taken my mind right up to the presence of the divine Subject, that in a moment the Eros from above [i.e. divine Love, as an attractive force] might carry me away and put me in an ecstatic unmediated contact with Him. This direct experience of His unmediated presence appears to me as light which fills everything.'[1] As the culminating union in love with the Blessed Trinity, such prayer brings human nature to the closest possible intimacy with God that is possible this side of the grave. The Light which the Trinity radiates in this union with the soul is indescribably powerful, which is why, to evoke it, Byzantine and post-Byzantine writers often draw the comparison with the accounts in the Synoptic gospels of the Transfiguration of Jesus and the icons that show

---

[1] Staniloae, *Orthodox Spirituality*, p. 343.

the apostles on Thabor shielding their faces as they slide down the mountain-side . The Light in question exists beyond our powers of conceptualization and imagination and yet, in Staniloae's phrase, it 'suggests concepts and images'.[2] Once this experience of union is terminated or at least suspended (because on earth it cannot be continuous, as Augustine had already grasped), the one who sees this Light may therefore try to express it, whether in concepts or images, not just for his own satisfaction but more especially for the sake of encouraging other people on the way to God. That is the origin of mystical reportage.

The Light is experienced as absolute fullness, the fullness of an 'inexhaustible reservoir of mystery',[3] and this means it is probably best described by the combined effort of a multiplicity of images, since such a combination is able to convey the sense of inexhaustibility. The eleventh-century Byzantine mystic St Symeon the New Theologian who identifies the Light in question as the Light of the love that God is, shed directly by the Holy Spirit, responds to it in Hymn 25 of his *Hymns of Divine Love* by just such a stream of images: 'O Drink of light! O Movement of fire! O Stirring of flames, which burn in me a sinner, which come from thy Glory! This Glory, I say it and I proclaim it, is thy Spirit, thy Holy Spirit, the Partaker of the same fire and glory with thee, O Word!' With this may be compared Richard Rolle's description of 'that fiery warmth, inestimably sweet' which, he says, 'can be heard and experienced only by one who has received it, and who must be purified and separated from the earth [so to

---

[2] *Ibid.*, p. 347.
[3] *Ibid.*, p. 350, note 333.

do]'.[4] The same images recur among authors who could not possibly have been aware of each other's texts, like Richard and Symeon, and this helps to attest the authenticity of the experience of divine Light that is claimed for the unitive way.

An Eastern contemporary of Rolle, the fourteenth-century Byzantine doctor Gregory Palamas, archbishop of Thessalonica, insists that the divine Light should be described neither as a material light nor as an intellectual light. It is entirely *sui generis*, unique to itself. He calls it a 'light of love beyond nature in which the very being of the one who sees it has been transformed'.[5] This transformation is the onset of deification, than which there is, even in heaven, no further goal. In its heavenly version, in the Age to Come, St Thomas will call what deifies or beatifies us, *lumen gloriae*, 'the light of glory'. It is the divinely intended outcome of that more occluded light, *lumen fidei*, 'the light of faith', which we know here and now, not least on the illuminative way.

Divine mystery

Before there is any question of looking further at any concepts or images in which union is expressed, it is useful to remind ourselves of how theologians have handled the concept of the mystery of God, with which at this point, obviously enough, we have supremely to do. It would be relevant, for instance, to cite some words of the German Jesuit theologian Karl Rahner from his last major work, *Foundations of Christian Faith*,

---

[4] Richard Rolle, *The Fire of Love*, XV.
[5] Staniloae, *Orthodox Spirituality*, p. 361.

about the non-disappearance of mystery in the knowledge of God, even in the Age to Come. 'Mystery ... is not something provisional which is done away with or which could in itself be non-mysterious. It is rather the characteristic which always and necessarily characterizes God, and through him characterizes us. This is so very true that the immediate vision of God which is promised to us as our fulfillment is the immediacy of the incomprehensible. It is, then, the shattering of the illusion that our lack of total comprehension is only provisional. For in this vision we shall see in God himself, and no longer merely in the infinite poverty of our transcendence that God is incomprehensible. But the vision of the mystery in itself, accepted in love, is the beatitude of the creature and it alone makes the One who is known as mystery the inconsumable thorn bush of the eternal flame of love.'[6] It might be added with von Balthasar that this mystery is not only to do with the hiddenness of the everlasting and unchanging divine Essence. It also concerns what von Balthasar terms the 'inconceivability' of what God has done for human beings in salvation history in the atoning work of his incarnate Son. Von Balthasar speaks of 'the overpowering and overwhelming inconceivability of the fact that God has loved us so much he surrendered his only Son for us, not only into creation, but emptied himself into the modalities of an existence [that is] determined by sin, corrupted by death and alienated from God',[7] a reference to the events of the Incarnation and the Atonement.

---

[6] Karl Rahner, *Foundations of Christian Faith*. English trans. (London: Darton, Longman and Todd, 1978), p. 217.

[7] von Balthasar, *The Glory of the Lord. A Theological Aesthetics. I. Seeing the Form*, p. 461.

That passage comes from the opening volume of von Balthasar's theological aesthetics, *The Glory of the Lord*. In an essay entitled 'Understanding Christian Mysticism', to be found in the fourth and last volume of his *Explorations in Theology*, he echoes it and also applies its message to the subjective appropriation of the Word in mystical experience:

> God's gesture in Jesus's Incarnation, Cross, descent into hell, Ascension to heaven cannot be plumbed but will always overflow with new mystery. I am 'seized' by it in an entirely objective understanding that can then also become subjective. God infuses his interiority in me in a manner that towers far above my human powers of sensation and feeling. So, in the very midst of Christian conversion, the ineffable is present. Only this time it is not set over against language any more [as the term 'ineffable' naturally suggests] but lies in the inner depths of theWord [i.e. the divine self-revelation] itself.[8]

Bouyer provides an entrée to what might be involved in such subjective appropriation of the inherently mysterious Word—specifically on the unitive way—by appealing to another doctrine especially associated with St Thomas. Comparing the three ways—purgative, illuminative, and unitive—he writes, 'If the purgative way was characterized by the extinction of the vices and the illuminative way by the development of the virtues (chiefly charity), then the unitive way can be defined by the predominance of the gifts of the Spirit'.[9] The 'gifts

---

[8] Hans Urs von Balthasar, 'Understanding Christian Mysticism', in *Explorations in Theology IV: Spirit and Institution*. English trans. (San Francisco: Ignatius, 1995), pp. 309–35, and here at p. 332. Translation slightly altered.

[9] Bouyer, *Introduction to Spirituality*, p. 276.

of the Spirit' — meaning there the Holy Spirit, the third Trinitarian Person — is the crucial phrase. It flags up a Thomistic way of thinking about mystical experience since, according to Thomas, the Gifts of the Spirit as listed in the Book of Isaiah (11:2), are 'wholly new and supernatural instincts of the soul' when compared with the virtues prescribed for the illuminative way.[10] When the *virtues* predominate in my life, the soul will manage to do well. But when the *Gifts* predominate in my life, then the soul will act spontaneously under the Holy Spirit's impulse — and this is far more. The French Neo-Thomist theologian Réginald Garrigou-Lagrange asked, 'What characterizes the mystical life?' He answered his own question, 'A special passivity or the predominance of the gifts of the Holy Ghost, having a superhuman mode specifically distinct from the human mode of the Christian virtues'.[11]

The Gifts in question are listed in the prayer with which the bishop asks for the Holy Spirit for candidates at Confirmation, and they make their way into most if not all Catechisms, Western and Eastern. But what is not normally done, outside the Thomist tradition, is to make the Gifts the essential key to Christian mysticism. An exception can be made for that winning nineteenth-century Russian saint, Seraphim of Sarov, when in his celebrated 'Conversation on the End of the Christian Life' he defined the aim of that life as the 'acquiring of the Holy Spirit'.[12]

---

[10] Ibid.
[11] Réginald Garrigou-Lagrange, *Christian Perfection and Contemplation according to St Thomas Aquinas and St John of the Cross*. English trans. (St Louis, MO: Herder, 1937), p. 162.
[12] Lossky, *The Mystical Theology of the Eastern Church*, p. 195. The gist of the 'conversation' is given at pp. 227–31.

Bouyer stresses that the diversity of the Gifts (six in the Hebrew text, seven in the Septuagint's Greek) is not the most important thing about them.[13] More important is the way the Gifts constitute *overall* a new quality of life for the soul, a quality of life which—extraordinary as it may seem to claim this—is nothing less than *the life of God himself in the soul*. Here the activity of the Spirit makes possible an experience so marvellous that the writers of the spiritual Tradition have to search hard to find words in which to stammer.

Concepts and images

Thus for instance, the twelfth-century monastic theologian William of St Thierry speaks of it as *unitas spiritus*, the unity—and not just union—between our spirit and the Holy Spirit of God. St Teresa speaks of it as the 'spiritual marriage', and so takes up a theme first introduced by Origen in his commentary (and two homilies) on the Song of Songs, and repeated by St Bernard of Clairvaux in his own sermons on the same Old Testament book, so admired in the mediaeval period for its evoking of loving union with God, all our 'spiritual senses' set a-tingle.[14] In St John of the Cross's text *The Spiritual Canticle* (the third of his four

[13] Bouyer might have referred to Thomas Aquinas, *Summa theologiae*, Ia. IIae., q. 68, a. 5, where he speaks of the Gifts as given together with charity as a unitary whole. This should not be supposed to mean that one or another Gift cannot predominate in this or that holy life, and this is how Catholic hagiography generally understands matters. See, for instance, Ambroise Gardeil, OP, *The Gifts of the Holy Spirit in the Dominican Saints*. English trans. (Milwaukee, WI: Bruce, 1937).

[14] Ann Astell, *The Song of Songs in the Middle Ages* (Ithaca, NY: Cornell University Press, 1990); E. Ann Matter, *The Voice of*

great works on the mystical path, following on *The Ascent of Mount Carmel* about the purgative way and *The Dark Night* about the illuminative way[15]), Teresa's fellow-Carmelite follows Bernard's lead. In *The Spiritual Canticle* John describes the unity at stake on the unitive way in matrimonial, or 'nuptial', language, just as St Teresa does.

However, in the last of his quartet of books, *The Living Flame of Love*, St John, while accepting there is no state to which on earth one can aspire more intimate than the spiritual marriage, describes how love—which, after all, is the heart of human marriage—can nevertheless itself grow deeper and become more ardent. To express this, he changes the imagery used hitherto. In *The Living Flame of Love* the central imagery is of a log of wood placed on a fire. Increasingly the log absorbs the light and heat with which the fire burns, yet in itself—in the application of the image to the union of God and the soul—the log is not consumed, it is not reduced to ash. Identifying the living Flame as the Holy Spirit, the Spirit of the Bridegroom, Jesus Christ, he speaks of the log becoming one with the fire in the depths of God.[16] This is the 'transforming union' which on St John's analysis of the mystical life is the ultimate terminus and goal.

    my Beloved: The Song of Songs in Western Medieval Christianity (Philadelphia: University of Pennsylvania Press, 1990).

[15] Unlike Evagrius, John's text for 'beginners', *The Ascent of Mount Carmel*, presumes 'dedicated individuals who have already resolutely decided to direct their lives to God'; he 'gives no attention to "pre-evangelization" or to the early stages of catechetical and spiritual training', Leonard Doohan, *The Contemporary Challenge of John of the Cross. An Introduction to his Life and Teaching* (Washington, DC: ICS Publications, 1995), p. 63.

[16] Ibid., p. 41.

Incidentally, the last poetic stanza around which John of the Cross arranges *The Living Flame* speaks not only of the individual person's communion with the Father's Word by the Spirit but also of 'experiencing the whole created cosmos in God'.[17] For St Maximus, as interpreted by Staniloae, delight in the created *logoi* will accompany even the final vision of God in heaven.[18]

Transformation

On the unitive way we have to come to terms with a unique experience of the grace of God, the uncreated Energies, as taking possession of our whole being. This transformation has been in prospect since our baptism, or, if one prefers, our justification, which normatively speaking belongs with sacramental Baptism. It has been in some form an aspect of any Christian life worth the name. Now, however, it predominates. It is the resurrection coming at last via the Cross. Extraordinary psychological experiences such as visions, ecstasies and the like have sometimes been recorded in connexion with such transformation but in no sense are they necessary accompaniments of it. Many mystics have not known these experiences, and as a general rule, nothing of this sort seems to take place any longer at the ultimate stage of the unitive way. Citing the Letter to the Galatians, 'I live, but no longer I, but Christ lives in me' (Galatians 2:20), von Balthasar adds an important caution to any preoccupation with experiences. 'The degree of one's awareness of this mystery remains a matter of indifference for the Christian life of

---

[17] *Ibid.*
[18] See Staniloae, *Orthodox Spirituality*, p. 204.

faith. What matters is that the Bride surrenders herself selflessly. She does not enquire after how much *she* experiences in the encounter, how the Bridegroom is accepting her, but whether he finds in her what he wishes.'[19] In spiritual theology, it is not necessarily a good idea to put the emphasis on experience, not even when someone is saying how divine grace takes human experience into a mode that goes beyond the human. Spirituality is not about me and my experience. It is about what God offers, and it asks, with what generosity have I responded? It is about the Word who invites.

---

[19] von Balthasar, 'Understanding Christian Mysticism', p. 335.

Bibliography

Anson, Peter F., *The Call of the Desert* (London: SPCK, 1973, 2nd edition)
Arintero, John G., OP, *The Mystical Evolution in the Development and Vitality of the Church*, 2 vols. (Rockford, IL: Tan Books, 1978 [1951])
Astell, Ann, *The Song of Songs in the Middle Ages* (Ithaca, NY: Cornell University Press, 1990)
von Balthasar, Hans Urs, *Explorations in Theology IV: Spirit and Institution*. English trans. (San Francisco: Ignatius, 1995)
—— *The Glory of the Lord. A Theological Aesthetics. I. Seeing the Form*. English trans. (Edinburgh: T. & T. Clark, 1982)
—— *Prayer*. English trans. (San Francisco: Ignatius, 1986)
Bedouelle, Guy, OP, *Saint Dominic. The Grace of the Word*. English trans. (San Francisco: Ignatius, 1987)
Bouyer, Louis, *Introduction to Spirituality*. English trans. (London: Darton, Longman and Todd, 1961); also published as *Introduction to the Spiritual Life* (Notre Dame, IN: Ave Maria Press, 2013)
—— *The Spirituality of the New Testament and the Fathers* (London: Burns and Oates, 1963)
Butler, Cuthbert, OSB, *Western Mysticism. The Teaching of SS. Augustine, Gregory and Bernard on Contemplation and the Contemplative Life* (London: Constable, 1927, 2nd edition)
Cabasilas, Nicholas, *The Life in Christ* (London: Janus, 1995 [1989])
Casel, Odo, *The Mystery of Christian Worship*. English trans. (New York: Crossroad, 1999)

Daniélou, Jean, *The Bible and the Liturgy* (Notre Dame, IN: University of Notre Dame Press, 1956)

Doohan, Leonard, *The Contemporary Challenge of John of the Cross. An Introduction to his Life and Teaching* (Washington, DC: ICS Publications, 1995)

Dupré, Louis, and Don E. Saliers (eds.), *Christian Spirituality. Post-Reformation and Modern* (London: SCM, 1990)

Foster, David, OSB, *Reading with God. Lectio Divina* (London: Continuum, 2005)

Garrigou-Lagrange, Réginald, *Christian Perfection and Contemplation according to St Thomas Aquinas and St John of the Cross*. English trans. (St Louis, MO: Herder, 1937)

—— *The Three Ages of the Interior Life: Prelude of Life Eternal*, 2 vols. English trans. (St Louis, MO: Herder, 1947–8)

Higgins, John J., SJ, *Merton's Theology of Prayer* (Spencer, MA: Cistercian Publications, 1971)

Johnston, William, *Christian Mysticism Today* (London: Collins, 1984)

Kadloubovsky, E., and G. E. H. Palmer (tr.), *Writings from the Philokalia on Prayer of the Heart* (London: Faber and Faber, 1951)

Knowles, David, *The English Mystical Tradition* (London: Burns and Oates, 1964 [1961])

—— *What is Mysticism?* (London: Burns and Oates, 1967)

Leclerq, Jean, *The Love of Learning and the Desire for God*. English trans. (New York: Fordham University Press, 1974, 2nd edition)

Lossky, Vladimir, *The Mystical Theology of the Eastern Church*. English trans. (London: James Clarke, 1957; reprinted Crestwood, NY: St Vladimir's Seminary Press, 1974)

Louth, Andrew, *Denys the Areopagite* (London: Geoffrey Chapman, 1989)

—— *The Origins of the Christian Mystical Tradition* (Oxford: Clarendon, 1983)

—— *The Wilderness of God* (London: Darton, Longman and Todd, 2003, 2nd edition)

Mantzarides, Giorgios L., *Orthodox Spiritual Life*. English trans. (Brookline, MA: Holy Cross Orthodox Press, 1994)

Matter, E. Ann, *The Voice of my Beloved: The Song of Songs in Western Medieval Christianity* (Philadelphia, PA: University of Pennsylvania Press, 1990)
Mazza, Enrico, *Mystagogy. A Theology of the Liturgy in the Patristic Age*. English trans. (New York: Pueblo, 1989)
McGinn, Bernard, *The Foundations of Mysticism. Origins to the Fifth Century* (New York: Crossroad, 1991)
—— *The Growth of Mysticism. Gregory the Great through the Twelfth Century* (New York: Crossroad, 1994)
——, John Meyendorff and Jean Leclerq (eds.), *Christian Spirituality: Origins to the Twelfth Century* (London: SCM, 1989)
Merton, Thomas, *Bread in the Wilderness* (London: Hollis and Carter, 1954)
A Monk of the Eastern Church [Lev Gillet], *Orthodox Spirituality* (London: Fellowship of SS Alban and Sergius, 1974)
Mouroux, Jean, *I Believe. The Personal Structure of Faith*. English trans. (New York: Sheed and Ward, 1960)
Nichols, Aidan, OP, *Deep Mysteries. God, Christ and Ourselves* (Lanham, MD: Lexington Books, 2018)
—— 'The Spirituality of the Dominicans', in his *Scribe of the Kingdom. Essays on Theology and Culture* (London: Sheed and Ward, 1994), II, pp. 199–206
—— *A Spirituality for the Twenty-First Century* (Huntington, IN: Our Sunday Visitor, 2003)
Rahner, Karl, *Foundations of Christian Faith*. English trans. (London: Darton, Longman and Todd, 1978)
Raitt, Jill, Bernard McGinn and John Meyendorff (eds.), *Christian Spirituality. High Middle Ages and Reformation* (London: SCM, 1989)
Schmemann, Alexander, *Of Water and the Spirit* (Crestwood, NY: St Vladimir's Seminary Press, 1974)
—— *The Eucharist, Sacrament of the Kingdom* (Crestwood, NY: St Vladimir's Seminary Press, 1988)
Staniloae, Dumitru, *Orthodox Spirituality. A Practical Guide for the Faithful and a Definitive Manual for the Scholar*. English trans. (South Canaan, PA: St Tikhon's Seminary Press, 2002)

Stolz, Anselm, *The Doctrine of Spiritual Perfection*. English trans. (St Louis, MO: Herder, 1948)

Torrell, Jean-Pierre, OP, *Saint Thomas Aquinas. Volume 2, Spiritual Master*. English trans. (Washington, DC: Catholic University of America Press, 2003)

Tsakiridis, George, *Evagrius Ponticus and Cognitive Science. A Look at Moral Evil and the Thoughts* (Eugene, OR: Pickwick, 2010).